Leading Cities

Leading Cities

A Global Review of City Leadership

Elizabeth Rapoport, Michele Acuto
and Leonora Grcheva

First published in 2019 by
UCL Press
University College London
Gower Street
London WC1E 6BT

Available to download free: www.ucl.ac.uk/ucl-press

Text © Authors, 2019
Images © Authors, 2019

The authors have asserted their rights under the Copyright, Designs and Patents Act 1988 to be identified as authors of this work.

A CIP catalogue record for this book is available from The British Library.

This book is published under a Creative Commons 4.0 International license (CC BY 4.0). This license allows you to share, copy, distribute and transmit the work; to adapt the work and to make commercial use of the work providing attribution is made to the authors (but not in any way that suggests that they endorse you or your use of the work). Attribution should include the following information:

Rapoport, E. et al. 2019. *Leading Cities: A Global Review of City Leadership*. London: UCL Press. https://doi.org/10.14324/111.9781787355453

Further details about Creative Commons licenses are available at
http://creativecommons.org/licenses/

ISBN: 978-1-78735-547-7 (Hbk)
ISBN: 978-1-78735-546-0 (Pbk)
ISBN: 978-1-78735-545-3 (PDF)
ISBN: 978-1-78735-548-4 (epub)
ISBN: 978-1-78735-549-1 (mobi)
ISBN: 978-1-78735-550-7 (html)
DOI: https://doi.org/10.14324/111.9781787355453

Contents

List of figures and tables	vi
List of authors	vii
Foreword	ix
Abha Joshi-Ghani and Greg Clark	
Acknowledgements	xiii
1. Introduction: a time for city leadership	1
2. Exploring city leadership: catalysts of action	11
3. The shape of leadership: actors and structures	35
4. Setting priorities: local leadership in a global world	59
5. Setting directions: leadership and strategic urban plans	76
6. Conclusion: a search for better city leadership	97
Appendices	103
References	111
Index	119

List of figures and tables

Figure 1.1	Cities included in the survey	7
Figure 2.1	Networking city leadership: growth in numbers of city networks per year	23
Figure 2.2	Elements of city leadership	33
Figure 3.1	Key themes addressed by city networks per period	37
Figure 3.2	City government structures by region	40
Figure 3.3	The 90 most networked cities by international city network membership	41
Figure 3.4	Government structures and their effectiveness	43
Figure 3.5	Leader's gender by region	46
Figure 3.6	Leaders' mandate	47
Figure 3.7	Leader effectiveness by mandate	48
Figure 4.1	Challenges cities will face in the next 10 years, as identified by survey respondents	60
Figure 5.1	Status of SUPs by region	83
Figure 5.2	Strategic urban plan effectiveness	84
Figure 5.3	Most frequently mentioned themes in SUP objectives	88
Figure 5.4	SUPs and evidence of coordination with other levels of government	90
Figure 5.5	SUP links to other plans	91
Figure 5.6	Organisations leading the plan development process	92
Figure 5.7	Partners in SUP processes	93
Figure 5.8	Organisations involved in the plan development process and project implementation	94
Table 4.1	Top categories of challenges cities will face, as discussed by survey respondents	61
Table 5.1	Documents reviewed for this research	85

List of authors

Elizabeth Rapoport is Director, Research and Advisory Services for the Urban Land Institute Europe, and an honorary lecturer in the Department of Science, Technology, Engineering and Public Policy at UCL (UCL STEaPP). In her previous role as a post-doctoral researcher at STEaPP, Elizabeth led a number of urban research projects on city leadership and urban governance, while her doctoral research focused on the international mobility of ideas about how to plan cities more sustainably. Her professional experience also includes time as a strategic and urban planning consultant with Buro Happold Engineering, and working on housing policy and strategy for the governments of both New York City and London and a London-based housing association. She has authored a number of articles and book chapters on urban sustainability and the international mobility of urban policy and planning ideas. She holds a Doctorate in Urban Sustainability and Resilience from UCL, and a MSc in Regional and Urban Planning Studies from the London School of Economics.

Michele Acuto is Professor of Global Urban Politics and Director of the Connected Cities Lab in the Faculty of Architecture, Building and Planning at the University of Melbourne. Michele is also a non-resident Senior Fellow of the Chicago Council on Global Affairs and a Senior Fellow of the Bosch Foundation Global Governance Futures Program. Michele was Director of the UCL City Leadership Lab and Professor of Diplomacy & Urban Theory at UCL, having previously worked as Stephen Barter Fellow of the Oxford Programme for the Future of Cities at the University of Oxford. He also taught at the University of Canberra, the University of Southern California, the Australian National University and the National University of Singapore. Outside academia, Michele worked for the Institute of European Affairs in Dublin, the International Campaign to Ban Landmines (ICBL), the Kimberley Process for conflict diamonds and the

European Commission's response to pandemic threats. Michele holds a PhD from the Australian National University.

Leonora Grcheva works as a community engagement and participation expert with UK company Soundings, leading the public consultation on large-scale planning and regeneration projects. She has previously worked as a planning consultant for the UN-Habitat Urban Planning and Design Lab in Nairobi, an integrative facility that supports local governments across the world to develop implementable design and policy projects, coordinating the spatial, economic and legal aspects of urban development. She has worked on urban plans and policies in Macedonia, UK, Ghana, Somalia and South Africa. Leonora has focused on different aspects of urban governance, both as a practitioner and as a researcher. She holds a PhD in Urbanism from the IUAV University in Venice, Italy.

Foreword

This important book investigates a critical imperative. Urbanisation is an accelerating global process, and cities are now the defining organisational units of our time. Yet we have learned very little, beyond anecdote, about what effective city leadership is. This matters deeply. If the promise of global urbanisation is that it can alleviate poverty, reduce carbon emissions, advance productivity and increase resilience security, then whether that promise is ever realised, city by city, will depend in large part on how the cities are led, managed, championed and reformed.

Good urbanisation may well turn out to be primarily an outcome of good city leadership, and bad urbanisation the product of poor city leadership. This is where 'urban studies' meets 'management science'. To address the issues embedded in this formula Elizabeth Rapoport, Michele Acuto and Leonora Grcheva first clear some significant conceptual ground. They start with the diversity of types and forms of cities. Not all cities are the same, and they inherit very distinctive institutional frameworks and resource bases. A deliberate focus of this book is to engage a very broad range of cities and move beyond the 'superstar' cities that are already much discussed. Large cities are not the same as small cities, mature cities have well-defined governance arrangements compared to new cities, cities in the emerging world work differently to those in developing countries, and each nation has a unique 'constitutional settlement' (the legal, fiscal and institutional standing of its cities) under which its cities operate. These specificities determine which political and financial powers cities have, and what governance arrangements they accrue.

The 'agreed' governance model for each city is an important determinant of what kinds of leadership it may need. Strong mayoral systems versus weak mayoral systems; councils versus commissions; agencies or authorities – each requires distinct leadership approaches and styles.

The second important insight is about how city leadership functions. As leadership is about effects on 'the led' as well as the actions and decisions of the leaders, there is a rich discussion of how citizens, urban society, networked governance and city leadership interact. City leadership, measured by its impacts, is about social behaviours, consumed services, civic society initiatives, organisational alignment and leveraged co-investment. Leadership of the city rests upon a culture of influence and storytelling. The extent to which city services meet the dynamic changing needs of citizens and visitors, and how such services evolve and change, is partly about how city leadership manifests itself and garners support. What stories are told and by whom, and how these narratives frame the vision and aspirations for the city, is a critical leadership function.

The authors also uncover and reveal critical insights about the shapes and sizes of cities. They observe the need for leadership of the 'functional city' rather than just the 'municipal city'. They examine the extent to which city leadership, governance and strategic planning operates at a metropolitan scale. Metropolitan areas, city-regions, urban-regions, become the focus of the narrative rather than narrowly defined municipal or administrative areas. The authors observe that the fragmented governance of the functional city leads to a dispersed and distributed system of leadership that involves not one but multiple city leaders, producing the requirement for convening activities between them. Leading the leaders turns out to be a fundamental challenge today.

Importantly, there are rich discussions on two other key issues: leadership of the future city and the collective leadership of cities as global force. An intriguing chapter addresses the role of strategic urban planning in cities. How can cities effectively plan a future, guided by long-term trends but rooted in current citizen values and choices, to set in motion a multi-cycle 'direction of travel'? This chapter helps the reader understand how an emerging form of collaborative and deliberative long-term strategic planning acts to shape a sense of possible urban and metropolitan futures. It shows how such planning can guide cross-party consensus on the future of the city to minimise the risk of erratic policy changes that hinder progress on long-term development issues. The city that thinks long term can act across the political divide coherently, and develop 'through cycle' interventions that avoid the ruptures of short-term political mandates.

Another important theme addresses the role of cities as a new force in global governance. How are cities acting together through joint leadership to impact on social inclusion, climate change, resilience, trade, investment, technology, data and global public health? What is now a well-established practice of 'urban advocacy' or 'city diplomacy' is traced back to its origins in founding city networks, city summits and global partnerships. This develops the concept of the collective leadership of cities, and the role of cities in twenty-first century reform agendas at the international level.

Ultimately, the ground-breaking contribution of this book is the fact that it draws upon a unique survey of 200+ cities from six different regions of the world, embracing younger and older, smaller and larger, richer and poorer cities. This gives the book a special resonance and purpose. It provides not just a global perspective, but it also helps to root the discussion in the huge diversity of cities that are evolving. The book creates a new benchmark in assembling such data and it provides a sound basis for future investigations.

City leadership in this varied context involves both 'formal powers of city management', and responsibilities, and the 'soft power of city leadership'; visioning, convening, networking, nudging and strategising. Social behaviours and how they are influenced by leadership are revealed as a new focus. The ability of city leaders, working together, to address global challenges is established as a new metric of global leadership.

There are three rather compelling implications that arise from this research. First, further research is needed on the state of city governance and the extent to which it is evolving in different locations to meet the needs of this urbanising century. Second, there is an opportunity to use this book to trigger a wider debate about the skills and attributes of city leaders. Third, universities, business schools and other teaching institutions should consider how they can help train and educate a wider base of people to contribute to the 'dispersed and distributed leadership' of cities that is a key insight in this text.

We all owe a debt of gratitude to the authors for their scholarly endeavour. Without this book we would have a much poorer sense of the key metrics that determine how ready our cities and city leaders are to realise the promise of our metropolitan century.

Abha Joshi-Ghani is the Senior Adviser and Head of Infrastructure Analytics and Programs for Infrastructure and Public-Private Partnerships at the World Bank. She is co-chair of the Global Future Council on the Future of Cities and Urbanization for the World Economic Forum, and former head of Global Urban Development Practice at the World Bank.

Greg Clark CBE is Honorary Professor at the UCL City Leadership Lab and Chairman of the Business of Cities Ltd, an urban intelligence group based at UCL. He is a global fellow at the Brookings Institution, LSE Cities and the Urban Land Institute.

Acknowledgements

'Cities' are a hot topic in world affairs. Mayors and coalitions of local governments are today active players in debates on topics ranging from global sustainability, resilience from disasters, climate action and inequality. The growing role of urban actors in tackling global challenges has attracted interest across media, business and academia, and often captures the public imagination. Yet while it seems that now, more than ever, is the time of city leadership, we also have very little systematic information on who leads cities around the world, and how they are led. *Leading Cities* is a response to the need for a broad, international and practical evidence base on city leadership and urban governance.

Starting in 2014, this book was developed as part of a broader research project funded by the UK's Economic and Social Research Council (ESRC) "Urban Gateways" grant on the role of cities in global governance, carried out by the UCL City Leadership Lab. The study that provides the foundations for this book was originally devised as a review of the state of city leadership internationally. In particular, it was designed with a view to the (at that time) impending Habitat III conference in Quito in October 2016 and the development of the United Nations (UN) New Urban Agenda. The original project informed the development of a suite of projects on city networks, crisis governance, city diplomacy and the role of cities in the UN.

As efforts towards an international cities agenda bloomed, we believed that, if we are to speak of the value of city leadership in responding to mounting challenges, we need an evidence base that goes beyond individual profiles, case studies and anecdotal evidence. Working with colleagues at the World Bank Group and at UN-Habitat, we developed a research approach that would lead to an 'arm's length' review of city leadership that 1) was global in nature, reaching out to cities big and small; 2) offered sympathetic critiques of a city's performance, relying on input by senior scholars rather than by cities themselves, and 3) applied an international comparative context to discussions of urban issues, places and trends, especially in relation to governance and planning.

Leading Cities and the *Urban Connections* programme rapidly expanded into a number of spin-off research projects for the UCL City Leadership Lab. As issues like city branding, networking, urban safety or natural hazards came to the fore, deeper dives and additional pathways opened up for us to explore city leadership. Yet the fundamental purpose of that project, to offer a thorough review of leadership, strategic planning and governance, remained at the heart of much of our work over the last four years.

The preparation of this book has been a long journey, and we are grateful to the many colleagues and institutions who helped us along the way.

The project was first funded by the ESRC via a Future Research Leaders grant supporting our time and research efforts. It was devised in collaboration with the then World Bank Institute and the United Nations Human Settlements Office's (UN-Habitat) Programmes Division. Thanks to Juma Assiago and Alioune Badiane at UN-Habitat for their support, even if that collaboration eventually veered more explicitly towards the safer cities agenda. Two of the world's foremost experts on city leadership, Greg Clark at the Business of Cities and Abha Joshi Ghani at the World Bank, offered insight, advice, encouragement and mentoring to the authors throughout the project for which we are extremely grateful. Portions of this research were also carried out at the University of Oxford Programme for the Future of Cities and the Faculty of Architecture, Building and Planning at the University of Melbourne, where this project eventually informed the establishment of the Connected Cities Lab. We are grateful for the support of these institutions and their staff.

A team of terrific researchers in the City Leadership Lab formed much of the backbone of this endeavour. They tirelessly unpacked the localised specificities, tricky differences and at times conflicting information telling us how city leadership was (and is) doing in places near and far. They did so regardless of having been assigned a major global metropolis or an unknown tertiary hub far away from their desks, always in a collegial vein, and trusting the goal was worth the effort. For this we are in debt to Charlotte Barrow, Alice Sweitzer, Yu-Shan Tseng, Asaf Frances, Katrien Steenmans, Marco Trombetta, Yvonne Yap, Hugo Decramer, Terry Jones, Jack Doughty and Mika Morissette.

Our sincere thanks also go to colleagues in UCL's Department of Science, Technology, Engineering and Public Policy (STEaPP), the home of the Lab, who supported us throughout the project and offered their expertise as we made our way through this work. In particular, we owe some special thanks to Ellie Cosgrave, Andrew Chilvers, Jean Paul Addie, Lily Song, Rocio Carrero, and also to Tim Moonen at the Business of Cities. Thanks to Suzanne Namer-Waldenstrom, Lourdes Garcia and Steve Morrison at STEaPP are also due for their patience in managing the project and us amid all sorts of scholarly and organisational challenges.

Leading Cities would have not been possible without the voluntary input of 292 scholars from all over the planet. Their time, input, critiques, support and expertise on leadership and governance in 202 cities was the backbone of our large comparative research exercise. Their contribution also speaks to a deeper theme we pick up in the conclusion of the book: academia can play as important a role as city leaders themselves, offering critical but also evidence-based insight into the state of city leadership and how to improve it. To maintain confidentiality, we have not included a full list of the experts who took our survey, but would like to offer our most sincere thanks and appreciation to all of them for sharing their time and expertise with us.

Last but not least, our thank you also goes to Chris Penfold and UCL Press for their patience with the lengthy development of this volume and for the opportunity to publish *Leading Cities* as an open and freely accessible volume – a format we hope will allow this global review to make its way into many of those cities we reached out to beyond the privileged North.

1
Introduction: a time for city leadership

Cities are home to the majority of the world's population, drivers of both national and global economic activity, hubs of culture and innovation, and are the locations in which many of society's greatest challenges, from climate change to social unrest, play out. Given this, it is not surprising that, in recent years, cities have captured the global imagination. A focus on cities and urban issues is now a common feature across business, politics and culture. As cities have become more visible, so too has the role of city leadership, from calls for mayors to 'rule the world', to sizeable philanthropic investments directly into supporting cities to improve their leadership capacity. Meanwhile, cities are no longer focusing only on activities within their own boundaries, but are seeking a greater voice and influence in tackling national and international challenges. Mayors are making strong statements and taking action on issues normally beyond their remits, such as natural disasters, immigration and climate change, often standing up against regional and national political leaders in the process. Despite this, we have relatively little data to underpin our understanding of city leadership and, in particular, to make meaningful comparisons between cities. Who leads cities and what political structures underpin this leadership? If we live in the age of the city, knowledge about who leads them, how they are governed and how they set strategic priorities is essential. This book is a first attempt to fill this gap.

City leadership: global agendas

In December 2015, speaking before international audiences and press on the eve of the negotiations that would lead to the Paris Agreement on Climate Change, Paris mayor Anne Hidalgo embodied many of the aspirations of city leadership today. Hidalgo spoke alongside former New York City mayor Michael Bloomberg, the newly appointed UN special envoy for cities and climate change, as well as philanthropists, business leaders, community activists and diplomats. Their speeches highlighted the centrality of city leadership in times of profound global transformations. Mayor Hidalgo, who was speaking just weeks after the terrorist attacks that had shaken Paris, was emblematic of the growing role of cities on the front lines when tackling issues of international importance, from climate change to terrorism.

This occasion was not unique. Indeed, 2015 and 2016 witnessed what we could call an 'urbanisation' of international multilateral negotiations and accords (Barnett and Parnell, 2016; Revi, 2016). The Paris Agreement came shortly after the agreement of the United Nations Sustainable Development Goals (SDGs). In a departure from conventional practices in international development, a coalition of actors managed to lobby successfully for an urban SDG ensuring an international target designed to promote safety, resilience and sustainability in cities. Also in March 2015, in the Japanese city of Sendai, diplomats agreed a new UN Framework on Disaster Risk Reduction, the 'Sendai Framework'. This framework took inspiration from the devastations of the 2011 Fukushima disaster, but also from recent disasters that had profound impacts on cities and their inhabitants in particular: Hurricane Katrina in 2005 and the 2010 earthquake in Port au Prince. In July 2015, the Addis Ababa Action Agenda for financing sustainable development forged an enhanced global partnership to foster equitable investment mechanisms (Parnell, 2018). Time and again, at each of these key milestones, city leadership emerged as central to the future of humanity and the response to some of today's most momentous challenges.

This was a feeling that reverberated throughout 2016, in the lead up to the third instalment of the United Nations Conference on Housing and Sustainable Urban Development (referred to as Habitat III) in October. Habitat III embodied the aspirations of an international community that has progressively been seduced by cities but also struggles to understand the intricacies of urban development and is confronted by important political questions. The legacy of Habitat III, a once-in-twenty-years occurrence in the UN System, is a 'New Urban Agenda' for the United Nations that promises to harness the transformative power of cities, building sustainable urban environments that can serve as engines of prosperity and centres of cultural and social well-being (Parnell, 2016).

Perhaps the most defining images of Habitat III and the Paris Conference on Climate Change have been those of hundreds of mayors, shoulder-to-shoulder, issuing statements on the role of cities in world affairs. Events such as these have confirmed the role of mayors as important actors on the international stage. The growing international visibility of city leaders comes at a time when their leadership is sorely needed. In a popular *Time* column, just months after the Paris talks, American political scientist Ian Bremmer predicted a lack of leadership on a global stage to be the most defining challenge of the years ahead. 'In a world of emergencies' said Bremmer, 'leadership matters' (Bremmer, 2015). The experience and expertise of local leaders is increasingly critical in addressing problems of international importance. Their strong presence at these events indicates their willingness to engage in tackling global challenges, from climate change to sustainable development.

While this international engagement is important and eye-catching, city leadership is fundamentally linked to a local place and local issues. Speaking in front of global audiences, mayors have reiterated time and time again how their international commitments and efforts are linked to issues in their own cities. Away from these global stages, everyday city leadership requires attention to a range of pragmatic issues including ensuring affordable housing, managing waste and keeping the city safe.

As cities and their leaders take a growing role on these international stages, 'city leadership' has become a phrase that is frequently invoked by governments, businesses, academics, journalists and other commentators. Despite this, there is no agreed definition of what city leadership is and little systematic knowledge about the forms it takes, how it operates, how it is evolving and its relationship to governance at both a local and international level. If international actors wish to appeal to city leaders to help address global challenges such as those outlined above, this gap must be addressed. Doing so requires going beyond the small number of larger and 'global' cities, that are often the focus of urban scholarship, to examine a diverse cross-section of cities. It also demands much more careful attention to the local context in which urban governance occurs. Debate on issues like those described above may occur at a global and transnational level but change will occur by working through and within local leadership and governance structures in cities. It is time to take city leadership seriously, to appraise it systematically and to place it in the context of the urban politics of cities the world over.

The challenge of city leadership

Leadership is a topic of interest in a wide range of disciplines. It is one of the most commonly discussed themes in literature on business, management and organisational development (Bolden et al., 2003) and is also frequently addressed in disciplines including healthcare, psychology and education. The multitude of courses, schools, books and journals focused on the topic of leadership demonstrate the engagement of both academics and professionals with the topic. The topic of *city* leadership specifically, while less well known and theorised, has been addressed by scholars in urban and regional governance, politics and urban planning. However, as we note below, existing 'urban' applications of leadership theories and discourses fall short of offering a systematic, replicable and policy-relevant theory of *city* leadership.

There are today substantial differences both between and within disciplines in the way scholars conceptualise and study leadership. Political scientists often focus on politics and power relations, psychologists on the interpersonal interactions that occur in leadership processes and management scientists on the characteristics of effective individual leaders. Some authors restrict their studies to individual leaders, while others emphasise that leadership is more than simply the work of individuals. At the same time, authors in international studies (e.g. Curtis, 2016) but also increasingly in urban research (e.g. Oosterlynck et al., 2018), have turned to discussing the agency that cities have in relation to the global developmental agendas sketched above, often with limited attention given to the implications and underpinnings of leadership in the cities they see 'going global'.

Focusing on the *city*, rather than an organisation, as the entity to be led adds a new set of considerations to the study of leadership. Leadership in cities must take account of a complex and varied range of 'economic, social and cultural practices that coexist in densely occupied spaces' (Borraz and John, 2004: 110). Practices and people in cities are networked and interdependent, which means that actions have multiple and sometimes unpredictable effects. In addition, while a city is a defined location in space, it is influenced not just by forces within its own borders but also by regional, national and international issues and events. This complexity makes the study of city leadership fascinating but also challenging.

'The city' and 'leadership' are both terms that encompass a wide range of possible topics and approaches. In the next chapter, we review how the key concepts and debates of general leadership theory might shape a more systematic study of city leadership, and use this to build a conceptualisation of city leadership that is replicable, applicable and understandable by academics and practitioners alike.[1] We argue that leadership is a complex and non-linear process of driving action. It is distributed in nature, and it involves three main components: individuals, the structures that underpin them and the tools that connect the two. It takes place locally, in a situated context, but is in dialogue with wider spheres of governance at national, regional and multilateral scales. City leadership is ultimately a catalyst for action, if not more precisely a catalytic process that brings together multiple elements of urban governance to identify and act on strategic priorities for the future of a city.

Chapter 3 focuses on two of the elements of city leadership, actors and structures, presenting the research findings on individual city leaders and city government structures, their effectiveness, and their challenges. This is then followed in chapter 4 with a discussion of the major policy issues that leaders confront today on the ground, their relationship with the global challenges emerging from processes like Habitat III and the SDGs, and what these challenges mean for those who seek to 'lead' their cities. In chapter 5 we focus on one particular example of a tool/instrument of city leadership – the strategic urban plan – looking at how and where is it used, in what form, and how it contributes to effective city leadership. The concluding chapter reconsiders the value of this conceptualisation of leadership, and how we can build on the research findings to further develop a template for researching and evaluating city leadership.

Designing a global review

This book is based on two years of research conducted with funding from the UK's Economic and Social Research Council (ESRC) and in collaboration with the World Bank Group, linking to a collaboration for the Habitat III 'New Urban Agenda' process with the United Nations Office for Human Settlements (UN-Habitat), mainly carried out by researchers at the City Leadership Laboratory at UCL. The programme began in the run up to Habitat III and the growing calls for city leaders to take on a more prominent role on a global stage. In this context, it seemed critical to us to develop a truly global baseline of knowledge about the current state of city leadership around the globe. The project started with a broad but critical question: 'what is the state of city leadership today, and what challenges do city leaders face?'

In answering this question, we sought to gather a broad evidence base that would take into account the practices of both the global cities that are often the focus of comparative urban research as well as lesser known secondary, tertiary and even more peripheral cities. Building a global evidence base seemed to the research team and our partners to be critical in order to inform discussions about city leadership, both locally and on the international stage. In 2014 the Lab's research team set out to gather data that could offer a global overview of the leadership and strategic visions in a diverse cross-section of cities, in both emerging and established economies. Overall, this analysis draws on research into 202 cities in 100 countries around the world (see Figure 1.1). Undertaking a project of this breadth throws up numerous methodological challenges. In addressing these, the contribution of this research is not just its analysis and conclusions. The project also offers lessons about the practice of 'going global' when seeking to offer a landscape review across such a wide and inclusive set of cities.

This research project required going beyond major hubs like Paris and New York and their globally visible leaders, as well as beyond those cities seen in rankings produced by the likes of *The Economist* and *Financial Times*. The ethos behind the selection criteria for the target group of case studies was that comparative urban research should aim to incorporate the experiences of a diverse array of cities across both the Global North and South. In particular, we wished to gather viewpoints that might serve as alternatives to the well-known perspectives of heavily researched so-called 'global' and 'mega' cities. The team developed an initial list of 200 cities of varying sizes with a roughly equal distribution among regions of the world. The team grouped cities into six regions, based on the regions used by the World Bank. These were Europe and North America, East Asia and the Pacific (including Oceania), Latin America and the Caribbean, the Middle East and North Africa, South and Central Asia and Sub-Saharan Africa. One deviation from the World Bank approach was our grouping of North America and Europe. The team also included several 'outlier' cities, that were geographically isolated, such as island cities (e.g. Malé in the Maldives) and cities in remote regions of the world (Nuuk in Greenland), to further push the boundaries of the more common discussions of city leadership.

The research team gathered primary and secondary data on each city using a combination of an online survey and desktop research. We drew on sources outside the governments of the cities studied, in order to

Figure 1.1 Cities included in the survey.
Source: authors

gather a more independent perspective. Primary research consisted of a survey sent to recognisable academic experts with specialist knowledge of the leadership and governance processes in a particular city, rather than of the cities themselves. The team selected these experts based on their relevant understanding of a city's planning, governance or urban development challenges. These experts were largely academics, with a proven track record (i.e. peer reviewed publications) of research on the city in question, and were not affiliated with local government in the city they reported on. This independent expert base differentiates *Leading Cities* from many other studies available at present, which tend to rely on self-reporting by cities or, alternatively, conduct entirely desktop-based analysis at a distance. Reports based on voluntary self-reporting by local governments can suffer from a number of biases like overestimation, intentional blindness or narrow views but also offer a more partial angle on questions about efficacy and legitimacy which were raised in the survey for this project. On the other hand, purely desktop-based (and typically consultancy-driven) pieces of analysis also run the risk of passing unfair external judgements that are divorced from, and might overlook, critical local contextual issues and dynamics.

The survey asked experts for basic information on leadership and governance in their city of expertise, as well as their views on the critical issues for city leadership, the effectiveness of governance structure and the city's strategic plan (if it had one) in tackling these issues. This data informs portions of the analysis in chapters 3, 4 and 5.

For each city in the survey, the team contacted up to three experts with a request for information that could have also remained anonymous. After three unsuccessful attempts, the team substituted the case study for a different but comparable city (in terms of characteristics and geographical location). This occurred for just under 22 per cent of the original list of 200 cities, which eventually led to the final list of 202 cities above. Wherever possible within the time constraints of the project, the original selection framework was maintained. The team also used snowball sampling, asking research participants to identify additional cases and experts in order to expand the study. The survey asked respondents to identify any other cities (and relevant scholars) that they recommended the team include in the research. In a number of cases these suggestions were used to substitute for cities for which data could not be collected.

Overall, we received survey responses from 292 experts on 202 cities. Where respondents provided conflicting results on objective data (such as the gender of a mayor), the team fact-checked responses using secondary sources, as well as conducting a series of direct interviews with the experts to reconcile or clarify results. The team analysed the data using the qualitative data analysis software programme MaxQDA. Cross-tabulations were usually employed to run queries looking for interesting patterns in the data. To analyse free text responses, in particular the challenges identified by experts, we used content analysis. Using an inductive approach, we developed a series of codes to group challenges and allow us to aggregate responses by category. The chapters that follow draw on this analysis to present both a summary of the data collected as well as patterns that emerged from detailed qualitative analysis.

In addition to the survey, the team used desktop research, carried out by a team of five research assistants with relevant linguistic capabilities, to gather data from secondary sources such as the academic and policy literature. This portion of the research focused on gathering data that is publicly available, such as the characteristics of leaders (e.g. term length, gender) and the existence of a strategic urban plan. Further interviews with local experts added additional insights into interesting examples of city leadership in cities the world over.

Coupled with this, the research team also drew on a parallel study, led by one of the co-authors of *Leading Cities* and supported by a team of four researchers, that mapped the international dimension of city leadership. This study mapped the extent, variety and geographies of formalised collaboration by and for city leaders, or 'city networks'. These networks, which now number in the hundreds, are increasingly common practice and provide forums through which local governments collaborate to address international issues on themes such as climate change, resilience, culture and many other areas. Using desktop research validated by expert insight, this project mapped 202 city networks of international, regional and national extent, their activities, foci and operating structures, and linked this database analysis to in-depth secondary and interview material. Insights from this study, which offer a snapshot of the international connectivity of city leadership, are included in *Leading Cities* to illustrate the growing international dimension of city leadership.

The challenges of 'going global'

Attempting a study of this breadth involved a number of methodological challenges. Important limitations on this type of research are the language and communication barriers arising from the geographical spread of cities covered. While English is *lingua franca* in much urban research and policy, when casting an analytic net that goes much wider than the commonly studied global cities, language quickly became an issue. This is of course not a challenge unique to urban studies: as colleagues in the natural sciences have pointed out (Amano et al., 2016), the proliferation of English-based media outlets and even the emergence of Spanish as a common second language for scientific and policy communication have not eased the challenge of engaging with local needs and specialised demands. This is all the more an issue when considering that a programme of research such as ours attempted to reach out into many locations normally 'off the map' when doing urban research (Robinson, 2002).

In this sense, an additional difficulty emerged when identifying experts on some cities, in particular cities in Latin America and Africa. The approach we took, as discussed above, was to (either by snowballing sampling or desk analysis) identify a city expert on the basis of a sustained academic (publication) record on the city in question. However, the relative lack of scholarship on mid- and small-sized cities, particularly in the Global South, made this method more challenging for those cities outside North America and Europe that we wished to study. One result of this is an unequal distribution of cities across regions, with Europe and North America over represented. Despite this limitation, the cities included in the research still represent a diverse cross-section of experiences, and our pool of cities is one of the broadest currently available in internationally-accessible urban studies.

The breadth of the study, which included a large number of cities, meant we were able to only collect a limited quantity of data for each city. Many additional areas emerged through the project that no doubt deserve further exploration. Given this, we would encourage the reader to take this volume as a starting point for a conversation on city leadership which we hope to continue to foster in the years to come.

Notes

1. As we highlight throughout the volume, we do not imply that academia is divorced from city leadership and international processes. Rather, we take a cue from the activist community of scholars that have advocated for a greater scientific say in the future of cities in outlets like *Nature* and *Science* (McPhearson et al., 2016; Acuto et al., 2018) and this book aims to offer a 'bridging' volume purposefully geared to policy relevance.

2
Exploring city leadership: catalysts of action

There is no shortage of places to start from when writing about leadership. Countless books and articles, both academic and non-academic, address the subject. This vast canon of work on leadership is generally accompanied by a smaller body of work on the leadership of cities and places. However, there are important differences in the ways scholars approach leadership. Some focus on politics and power, others on interpersonal interactions, still others on the individual characteristics of effective leaders, while some emphasise that leadership is more than simply the work of individuals. As a result, there are a number of important choices to make when studying leadership that will shape the direction of the research and analysis. Focusing on the *city* as the entity to be led, rather than on an organisation, adds a new set of considerations to the study of leadership.

Before delving into our review of city leadership globally, this chapter takes stock of the options for analysing city leadership. We present the findings from a review of the substantial body of work on leadership and city leadership, then build on this to develop a practical theory of city leadership. This theory considers both the individual and structural aspects of city leadership, as well as the relationship between leadership and action on the ground in cities around the world. We argue that leadership is a process, one that it is 'distributed' not just individual, involving both individuals and the 'structures' that underpin them, and the 'tools' that connect the two. City leadership is a 'catalyst for action': a catalytic process that brings together multiple elements of urban governance to identify and act on city priorities.

Leadership: theory and traits

Much of the existing theoretical and empirical work on leadership tends to tackle two closely related issues: what leadership is and what constitutes effective leadership. Scholars have taken an array of approaches to answering these questions, sometimes with a focus on individual leaders and sometimes looking at the broader concept of leadership. In this section, we present a summary of how some of the most prominent and relevant theories of leadership answer these questions. However, a starting caveat is necessary here. Although *Leading Cities* is global in scope, the summary that follows reflects the dominance of North American and European scholars in the literature on leadership and city leadership. The vast majority of the most readily available and highly cited works on leadership still comes from these regions of the world, albeit an increasing number of papers are now coming from East Asia. As highlighted in literature on leadership that focuses on other regions of the world, findings from European/North American scholarship cannot be assumed to be universal (Jogulu and Ferkins, 2012; Kennedy, 2002; Mines and Gourishankar, 1990; Shatkin, 2004). We recognise that this is a limitation on the findings of this section. For this reason, and given the global logic of the framework in *Leading Cities*, the empirical sections of this book draw on a more diverse range of international experiences.

What is leadership?

A significant challenge when studying leadership is the sheer number of theories that exist. In an extensive literature review, Dinh et al. (2014) identified 63 distinct types of leadership theory. Among these theories there are a variety of different conceptions of what 'leadership' itself actually is. Leadership has sometimes been equated with management (Yukl, 1989) but, more recently, authors have begun to distinguish between management and leadership. Managers direct affairs, ensure their teams deliver services and meet targets, while leaders are more future-oriented and visionary, and work to create an environment that fosters innovation and inspiration (Iles and Preece, 2006; Zaleznik, 1977). This shift has reinforced a shift by researchers away from identifying effective leadership structures towards the properties of effective leaders and leadership processes.

Leadership can be seen as both a process and a property (Jago, 1982). Theories that focus on leadership as a property often equate leadership with the individual 'leader', something that is also a characteristic of much of the work on city leadership, as we will demonstrate below.

Leader-focused theories often attempt to identify the traits, behaviours and styles of individual leaders (Bolden et al., 2003; Horner, 1997). In doing so, they often focus on identifying the characteristics and capabilities of effective leaders, such as the capacity to motivate and inspire others (Palmer et al., 2001), or to be 'visionary' in setting goals (Zaleznik, 1977).

The notion of leadership as a process is the most common theme among the many definitions of leadership in the literature (Graen and Uhl-Bien, 1995; Hosking, 1988; Jago, 1982; Stogdill, 1950; Van Wart, 2013; Yukl, 1989). Specifically, leadership is frequently described as a process in which a leader exercises *influence* on others (usually an organised group) towards *the achievement of goals or objectives* (Hersey et al., 2007; Northouse, 2012; Stogdill, 1950; Tannenbaum et al., 1961; Yukl, 1989). The process of leadership, then, is one of social interaction that leads to change (Bass, 1990a; Bennis, 2007; Hosking, 1988; Naidu and Van der Walt, 2005; Tannenbaum et al., 1961; Uhl-Bien, 2006).

Theories of leadership vary in the way they describe the nature of the interactions between leaders and others, and thus vary in the understanding of precisely what leadership entails. Some classical definitions of leadership focus on the process through which a leader *directs* others (Prentice, 1961). More contemporary theories focus on the need for the leader to work in partnership with others (facilitative leadership, see Gains et al., 2007) or to motivate followers to exceed expectations (transformational leadership, see Bass, 1990b). The majority of leadership theories in current use describe leaders as exercising *non-coercive influence*; leaders motivate and inspire rather than direct (Jago, 1982; Palmer et al., 2001).

Focusing on the common threads in leadership theories provides useful insights but also obscures the many important debates and distinctions in the study of leadership. The next section briefly reviews some prominent theories of leadership before moving on to explicitly discuss theory and research on city leadership.

The sheer number and diversity of theories makes them difficult to categorise. In the following discussion we adopt a categorisation proposed by Graen and Uhl-Bien (1995), who group theories according to which of three 'domains' of leadership they focus on: leaders, followers, or the relationships between them. Leader- and follower-based approaches examine the traits, behaviours and attitudes of these two groups. Relationship-based approaches focus on the relationships between leaders and followers. As follower-based approaches are the least common, in the discussion below we focus on leader-based and relationship-based approaches.

Leader-based approaches: leadership as leaders

Much of the early work on leadership focused on leaders as 'gifted' individuals (Avolio et al., 2009; Billing and Alvesson, 1989; Bolden, 2011; Bolden and Kirk, 2006). Early 'Great Man' (sic) theories viewed leaders as exceptional people. This gave rise, first, to efforts to identify the traits of effective leaders (Bass, 1990a; Bolden et al., 2003). From the 1940s, trait-based approaches were replaced by a more behavioural approach to leadership research that focused on the actions of leaders rather than their personal characteristics (Papa et al., 2007). These 'style' approaches focused on the behaviour of leaders in their interactions with followers.

A significant shift in the study of leadership styles came with Fiedler's (1967) contingency model, which introduced the concept that the traits and behaviours that make leadership effective depend on context. A number of subsequent leadership theories, including situational, contingency and adaptive leadership, build on this observation. Such theories highlight that contextual factors, such as the type of situation or level of a follower's development, determine what style is most appropriate (Avolio, 2007; Bass, 1990a; Papa et al., 2007).

Dissatisfaction with a focus on the exchanges between leaders and followers led Bass (1990b, 1995) to distinguish between 'transactional' and 'transformational' leadership. Transactional leaders recognise and respond to follower needs and self-interests and reward good performance (Bass, 1990b; Purdue, 2001). Transformational leaders, by contrast, motivate followers to do more than would usually be expected, raise the awareness of followers about important matters and lead followers to transcend their own self-interests for the good of the team or organisation (Bass, 1997). The distinction between transactional and transformational leadership has since been taken up by numerous scholars of leadership in the private, public and non-profit sectors, as well as those studying leadership in cities (Avolio et al., 1999; Bass, 1990a; Carless, 1998; Palmer et al., 2001; Purdue, 2001; Rada, 1999; Wright and Pandey, 2010). Dinh et al.'s (2014) survey of the leadership literature found that transformational leadership was, by some margin, the most common focus in articles on leadership theory.

Common to the approaches outlined so far is the premise that leaders are seen as the source of leadership. The process of leadership, from this perspective, consists of the leader applying a set of skills and tools (such as communication, decision-making, negotiation and problem-solving) in order to catalyse change (Bolden, 2011). The focus on leaders brings with it clear normative implications for how to enhance leadership: focus on improving leaders and leaders' relationships with their followers. Today such leader- and leader-follower-based approaches inform most private and public sector leadership standards and competency frameworks (Bolden et al., 2003). Nevertheless, dissatisfaction with a focus on traits and styles of individual leaders has led to the development of a range of alternative theories, some of which are explored in the next section. These alternative relationship-based approaches highlight that the personal qualities of the leader are unlikely to be sufficient for the exercise of leadership.

Relationship-based approaches: leadership as a process

The individualistic approaches outlined above tend to see leadership in a hierarchical way, with a leader influencing followers (usually subordinates). Yet leadership is not the monopoly or responsibility of just one person: leadership relationships may also exist among peers and even across different organisations (Uhl-Bien et al., 2007). This is one of the principles underpinning relational theories of leadership. Relational leadership theorists see leadership as a process of social influence and take as their starting point processes rather than people (Hosking, 2007; Uhl-Bien, 2006).

Uhl-Bien (2006) divides relational leadership perspectives into two categories: entity and relational. Both take relationships and the process of leadership as their starting point. Entity perspectives (such as Leader-Member Exchange theory, see below), focus on the individuals within relationships; the process of leadership is largely about individuals influencing others. Relational approaches, by contrast, focus on the 'collective dynamic' of an organisation (Uhl-Bien, 2006: 662). Empirically, entity perspectives study the individuals involved in the process of leadership: their perceptions, attributes and behaviours (Dachler and Hosking, 1995; Uhl-Bien, 2006). Relational perspectives focus on social processes; the primary unit of analysis for leadership research becomes relationships rather than individuals.

Leader-Member Exchange (LMX) theory, which emerged in the 1970s, focuses on the leader, the follower and the different types of relationship between the two (Dienesch and Liden, 1986; Graen and Uhl-Bien, 1995; Liden et al., 1997). Empirical studies of leadership that apply an LMX approach go beyond the individual leader to focus on three domains of leadership: follower, leader and the relationships between them (Graen and Uhl-Bien, 1995). Prescriptions for effective leadership focus on developing and maintaining mature leadership relationships (Graen and Uhl-Bien, 1995).

One of the most prominent relationship-based approaches to leadership is distributed leadership, which has largely been developed in the literature on education and school leadership (Bolden, 2011; Gronn, 2000; Spillane, 2006). Distributed leadership is one of a family of similar concepts (e.g. shared leadership) that seek to shift attention away from individual leaders. From a distributed leadership perspective, leadership is not the monopoly or responsibility of just one person and there is a need for a more collective and more systemic understanding of leadership as a social process. Bennett et al. (2003: 7, cited in Bolden, 2011) summarise three shared premises of this approach: 1) leadership is an emergent property of a group or network of interacting individuals; 2) there is openness to the boundaries of leadership, and 3) varieties of expertise are distributed across the many, rather than a few.

A distributed approach goes beyond simply recognising that there are a large number of individuals beyond the recognised 'leader' involved in leadership, to a focus on leadership practice (Gronn, 2000; Spillane, 2006). Leadership practice consists of the *interactions* between leaders, followers and the context they operate in, and is therefore not fixed but fluid (Gronn, 2000). Leadership and context are reflexive, that is, context defines leadership practice but is also defined by it (Spillane, 2006). Empirically, applying a distributed leadership approach implies that studies of leadership should focus not on individual leaders, or structures of leadership, but on the practice of leadership and the interactions of the many individuals involved (Bennis, 2007; Hosking, 1988; Naidu and Van der Walt, 2005; Tannenbaum et al., 1961).

This is a very similar tenet to that of Complexity Leadership Theory (CLT), which similarly critiques the focus in leadership theory on individual leaders but proposes instead that leadership exists only in interactions. Building on complexity theory, which highlights the unpredictability but also the adaptability of systems, Uhl-Bien et al. (2007) propose that leadership interactions occur within Complex Adaptive Systems (CAS). Complex adaptive systems are more than just complicated:

> *'If a system can be described in terms of its individual constituents (even if there are a huge number of constituents), it is merely complicated; if the interactions among the constituents of the system, and the interaction between the system and its environment, are of such a nature that the system as a whole cannot be fully understood simply by analyzing its components, it is complex'* (Cilliers 2008, cited in Uhl-Bien et al. 2007: 299).

Building on Heifetz's theory of adaptive leadership (Heifetz, 1994; Heifetz et al. 2009), Uhl-Bien et al. (2007) propose that, in this context, leadership is about 'adaptive work' (adjusting to changes through learning, innovation or changing behaviour) rather than solving technical problems, thus not only involving adaptive leadership but also including an 'emergent' element to leadership which puts much emphasis on establishing the conditions for creative problem-solving. This focus is key because leaders, especially those in government (such as city leaders), are increasingly embedded in a wider system of politics beyond *government* – an observation that takes us to a more explicit focus on the 'place' of leadership in our book, i.e. in and for *cities*.

Understanding leadership in cities

The task of governing a city has, in modern times, largely been the responsibility of a municipal government, typically made up of an elected or appointed leader or leaders, and a professional bureaucracy. Increasingly, and in particular since the 1980s, the formal hierarchy of the state has been complemented by a range of other actors who are involved in setting priorities, delivering services and performing many other tasks key to governing an urban area. In short, the govern*ment* of cities has progressively evolved into a more complex landscape of urban govern*ance*.

From city government to city governance

The term *governance* is frequently used to describe this move away from a traditional, state-centred approach to governing (Palumbo, 2010; Stoker, 1998). Governance is defined in academia in a variety of ways but these diverse approaches all broadly imply a focus on informal horizontal networks over formal, vertical institutions (Borraz and John, 2004; Savitch and Vogel, 2009). Governance represents a move away from a top-down approach to governing, dominated by the nation-state, towards more complex (but not necessarily flat and equitable) political structures. The rise of informal networks and the growing participation of non-state actors in the activities of governing have led to a shifting role for the state. Rather than provider of services, government has become a strategic enabler of service delivery, managing through setting objectives rather than creating rules (Healey, 1997).

Governance does not replace government; rather the term aims to describe the more complex and flexible approach to public decision-making, where 'public decisions rest less within hierarchically organised bureaucracies, but take place more in long-term relationships between these key individuals' (Borraz and John, 2004: 112). Hence, for the purpose of this book, the Lab's research team has sought to define government as consisting of formal structures of elected or appointed leaders that are mandated to manage a city. Governance, on the other hand, is understood here as the wider spectrum of public and private actors involved in delivering public services, managing core services of the city and setting strategic priorities for its development.

In this context policy (making) networks are more open, complex and potentially unstable, opening up for a variety of stakeholders (not necessarily 'placed' in the city but also external to it) to affect the way the public domain and life in the city are shaped. This, while challenging the idea of a controlling local government governance also opens up multiple possibilities for city leadership as a catalyst in a fluid environment subject to change, coalitions and complexity.

In this sense, the shift towards governance in cities has led to a greater use of partnerships in the work of governing (Bassett, 1996; Lowndes and Skelcher, 1998). Local governments now work with a broad range of actors from across society to develop strategic priorities and deliver services. In debates about city leadership and urban governance, the roles of formal government and hierarchical approaches to governing are often debated, questioned and recast. One popular perspective is that effective governance requires retaining elements of a hierarchical system, with government remaining, to an extent, outside and 'above' governance arrangements (Kjær, 2004). Another emerging view is that governance is a task best undertaken by interdependent, interorganisational networks that are often largely autonomous. Furthermore governments should work among, and manage, the networks that govern (Rhodes, 1996, 1997).

Observing and studying the processes of governing cities from a 'governance perspective' requires attention to two core issues. First, a focus on society, in particular the relationship between society and the state, and the role of society in governing (Kooiman, 2003; Pierre and Peters, 2000). It is important to avoid detaching governing from those that are governed who are also, in many cases, those that select who will govern. Second, a governance perspective emphasises the role of networks (Kjær, 2004; Rhodes, 1997) and connections among the key actors (or 'stakeholders') shaping the geography of governance. Networks, in the realm of urban policy and governance, can be defined as 'stable patterns of social relations between interdependent actors which take shape around policy problems and/or policy programmes' (Kickert and Klijn, in Kickert et al., 1997: 6). These crystallised networks, through which collaboration occurs, lend stability to the fluid, complex world of urban governance.

Some of the stated benefits of governance, over more traditional command-and-control governing mechanisms, include increased innovation and efficiency (Kearns and Paddison, 2000). However, governance has also been critiqued as putting governing in the hands of unaccountable institutions, or making governments too beholden to business interests (Palumbo, 2010). Networks also have advantages and disadvantages. They offer flexibility and responsiveness but can also be difficult to control, lack durability, and incapable of coordinating a comprehensive response to a policy issue (Kjær, 2004).

For a study of city leadership, this emphasis on the role of society and networks in governing draws attention to the fact that city leadership is about far more than the individual leader who is often at the centre of political, economic and media attention. City leaders, as the chapters that follow will highlight, are one part of the process of city leadership. Exploring the role these leaders play, and how they interact with the other actors, structures and processes that influence the leadership of cities, is ultimately one of the main contributions this book seeks to make. Before turning the focus explicitly on leadership, the next section addresses the critical question of boundaries: where do we locate the 'city' being governed?

Geographies of governance: cities, regions and city-regions

All too frequently, we find, media, policy, business and even academia tend to simply point at 'cities' without being clear about what they are addressing. This is an important point because cities as defined by their administrative boundaries are not independent, autonomous units. Rather, they generally form part of a metropolitan region made up of a number of cities and towns (Scott, 2001a). Metropolitan regions are characterised by significant economic and social interdependencies, and often share responsibility for infrastructure and service delivery. In cities around the world, critical infrastructure such as public transport almost always operates at a regional scale. The regional dimension of urban life is an important consideration when thinking about city leadership and governance.

Among scholars of metropolitan and regional governance, there are two traditional theories of how to organise local governments: metropolitan government and polycentrism (Savitch and Vogel, 2009). A 'metropolitan government' approach holds that city boundaries, and governments, should encompass the entire metropolitan region. This can be achieved by consolidating smaller authorities, or creating a metropolitan government on top of existing, smaller, local governments. In contrast, the polycentric perspective holds that the market organises the most efficient provision and coordination of public services. From this perspective, local government fragmentation creates competition between municipalities for residents and businesses.

These different governance structures each have their advantages and limitations. In some academic circles it is broadly argued that smaller governments bring greater efficiency, access and accountability, while larger ones bring greater economies of scale, equity and regional coordination (Slack and Côté, 2014). Changes to formal institutions (such as the creation of metropolitan or regional government structures) are often connected in part to changes in thinking about the appropriate geographical scale for urban governance. Debates about the appropriate scale for urban governance are also increasingly influenced by the widely-held view that contemporary city-regions compete on the international stage, independently from their national government (Jonas and Ward, 2007; Scott, 2001b). To this end, contemporary arguments about the merits of particular forms of governance, in particular city-region or metropolitan governance, focus on their role in fostering economic growth and competitiveness (Deas, 2014; Savitch and Vogel, 2009).

In recent years, many cities have put in place some form of metropolitan governance structures. Research by the Organisation for Economic Cooperation and Development (OECD) into 263 metropolitan areas found that nearly two-thirds have some form of metropolitan governance body in place, with a substantial increase in their creation since the 1990s (Ahrend et al., 2014). The OECD has been prominent in investigating and promoting the link between metropolitan governance bodies and economic growth and investment. In a series of recent reports, it has argued that metropolitan governance bodies are associated with economic growth, unlock inward investment and promote well-being (Ahrend et al., 2014; OECD, 2015). One report found that city-regions with a metropolitan tier of governance in place tend to have higher per capita GDP, and they also perform better in areas such as public transport provision and controlling urban sprawl (Ahrend et al., 2014).

Leadership in a context of governance

The issue of leadership is an important component of many theories of urban governance. Perhaps the most prominent urban political theory of recent years, urban regime theory, examines how elected and civic leaders come together to form governing coalitions (Mossberger and Stoker, 2001; Stone, 1989). Regime theory highlights the networked and often informal nature of contemporary urban governance and leadership, in which business and community leaders develop informal but longstanding relationships with each other, city officials and politicians (Digaetano and Klemanski, 1999; Stone, 1989). Over time, informal relationships may be converted into more formal arrangements, as occurred recently in England with the creation of Local Enterprise Partnerships that bring together government, business and civic leaders to set city strategies (Deas et al., 2013).

A global trend towards the decentralisation of governance has led to an increased focus on local leadership (Borraz and John, 2004; Copus, 2008). Much of the empirical work on city leadership in recent years focuses on the impact of institutional forms and reforms on leadership style (Elcock, 2008; Fenwick and Elcock, 2005; Gains et al., 2007; Greasley and Stoker, 2008; Mouritzen and Svara, 2002; Svara, 2003). In Europe, and particularly the UK, this work has focused on the implications of local government reforms designed to give greater power and authority to local political leaders (Borraz and John, 2004; Evans, 2014). Both Europe and Latin America have seen a growth in the number of cities with elected mayors (Borraz and John, 2004; Montero and Samuels, 2004).

This focus reflects a recurrent theme in the European and North American literature: the need for city leadership to evolve. In order to adapt to the shift from government to governance described earlier, city leadership needs to become more distributive, and leaders need to facilitate rather than direct (Borraz and John, 2004; Gibney et al., 2009; Hambleton and Howard, 2013). Once again, despite the claims that cities are different from other organisations, organisational leadership theorists have also argued that changes in organisational forms require more distributed leadership (Bolden and Kirk, 2006).

The focus on institutional reforms is, in large part, introduced to tackle a crisis of legitimacy in local government, resulting from low electoral turnout in local elections and lack of accountability of local leaders (Borraz and John, 2004). One institutional change that is often associated with an increase in legitimacy is the introduction of a directly elected mayor. However, while institutional design can make a difference to leadership (Gains et al., 2007; Greasley and Stoker, 2008) there is no consensus in the literature on the 'best' design for improving legitimacy.

A discussion of city leadership needs, therefore, to be placed in the context of the closely related area of urban governance – a methodological consideration that shapes much of the inquiry in the following chapters. Governance provides the context within which city leadership occurs, while city leadership is a core element of governing cities. This is a dialectical two-way relationship: leadership at the same time shapes and is shaped by the very place in which it occurs. This, however, requires us to move even more explicitly to understanding how theories of leadership can be applied to the 'city'.

Leadership in a context of global urban governance

Leadership in cities takes place today not just in a context of decentralisation and the shift towards governance; the 'international' dimension of city leadership is also increasingly important. The challenges faced by city leaders, from air pollution to inequality to social unrest and the rise of populism, are increasingly intertwined with global challenges. Yet what does this mean practically when we seek to study the structures and actors defining city leadership the world over? First and foremost, this calls upon a more refined understanding and definition of what we mean by 'international' and what constitutes this sphere of politics as it relates to city leadership and governance.

City leaders, and the urban challenges they face, are embedded in a wider realm of global flows, institutions and politics. This includes the multilateral agencies, multinational companies and transnational networks that constitute the current architecture of world politics. The so-called 'international system' (Bull, 2012) plays a key role in urban politics today. This includes strategies and interventions by global multilateral agencies such as the United Nations, as well as the World Bank and the OECD. Regional-level international organisations also have a substantial impact on cities, most prominently within the European Union, but also in other regions through entities like the African Union, Caricom or the Association of South-East Asian Nations (ASEAN). While the activities of these international actors can have profound impacts on cities, the cities have a limited ability to influence them, with diplomatic relations and (international) legal frameworks largely managed at the national level.

Yet limiting our appreciation of the role of international agencies to the realm of states and international politics neglects critical elements of how international diplomacy and city leadership actually interact. Built around and across the 'skeleton' of the international system described above is a whole realm of 'global governance' (Weiss and Wilkinson, 2014) that includes private and not-for-profit actors, from corporations to foundations, which routinely play important roles in responding to urban challenges. Alongside these, there are also many transnational initiatives that bypass the formal international mechanisms but still cut across national boundaries to impact on cities. These include civil society movements such as Slum Dwellers International, global organisations of sub-national governments – including powerful city networks such as the Climate Leadership Group (C40) and the United Cities and Local Government (UCLG) – and hybrid networks and lobby coalitions that mix these actors. These all contribute to reshaping the political conditions in which city leadership is exercised beyond individual cities (Acuto, 2018; Curtis, 2018). As flagged in Figure 2.1 below, this is a growing reality for cities the world over, with upwards of four new networked partnerships emerging every year since the turn of the millennium.

All of this is leading to the emergence of a complex realm of governance of urban issues occurring at an international scale, or 'global urban governance' (Verrest et al., 2013; Acuto and Parnell, 2016). Building on this, there are several important elements that need to be taken into consideration in order to account for the 'international dimension' of city leadership. First, as noted above, that the formal multilateral system of UN agencies and international politics is just one part of a more complex network of actors operating at a range of regional and international

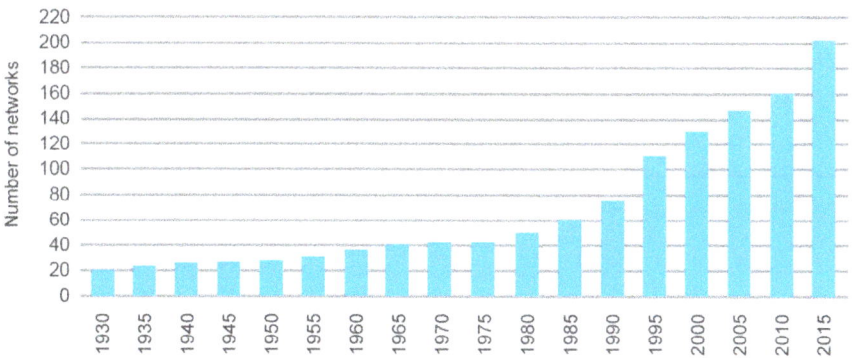

Figure 2.1 Networking city leadership: growth in numbers of city networks per year.
Source: authors

scales. Second, while these actors are not affiliated with nation-states (who remain the primary actors in formal diplomacy), they are linked to the international system through participation in and referencing of UN frameworks. Their participation may come through links with nation-states but may also come about in other ways. For example, support from other donors was pivotal in continuing the practice of holding side events and alternative or 'track 2' diplomatic encounters during the Habitat III process in Quito in 2016.

A third element, and an important shift, is that cities are now not just 'problems' or 'issues' to be addressed in international development. Rather, there is a growing recognition that local authorities are excellent partners and should be empowered. This principle was, for instance, embedded in the UN's Sendai Framework for Disaster Risk Reduction in March 2015 and in the establishment of universally binding Sustainable Development Goals (SDGs) in September of the same year. This was shortly followed by similar acknowledgements in the December 2015 Paris Agreement on Climate Change, successor to the Kyoto Protocol, and the Addis Ababa Action Agenda on financing sustainable development. All of these now much-cited frameworks push city leaders to engage with global issues, and in turn have been advocated for by city leaders who seek to extend their horizons beyond localised urban management priorities.

Fourth, over the last few decades the international system has witnessed a steady growth of new actors playing an important role in shaping and promoting urban leadership agendas. There has been a rapid growth in the number of city networks, i.e. organisations through which cities come together to share knowledge and agree common agendas for lobbying other actors. These networks now number in the hundreds and, in some cases, are moving considerable resources towards urban settlements even when international politics has taken a much slower pace (Acuto, 2016; Gordon and Johnson, 2017; Curtis, 2018). Perhaps even more markedly, the global growth of philanthropy and private investment in development has also shaped urban agendas big and small. Alongside these, international consultants, both large multinational firms and influential individuals, have taken an important role in defining urban priorities in both international frameworks and local contexts (Rapoport, 2015; Rapoport and Hult, 2017).

The final element to consider is the role of the nation-state as a more explicitly urban actor. Many countries have now begun creating 'National Urban Policies', and developing city-focused ministries, programmes and initiatives aimed at articulating the national scope of urban issues

(Dodson, 2017). Overall, this complex landscape has important implications for studying processes of development in cities as it pushes us not to treat all urban political issues as local but rather to consider urban governance, strategic planning and city leadership in dialogue with often complex international urban politics (Caprotti et al., 2017).

From leadership to place leadership

The study of city leadership is not a single field. The topic is addressed by scholars from a broad range of disciplinary perspectives, including political studies, planning studies, public administration and economic geography to name a few. Empirical studies have examined the changing role of leadership in the context of local government reform, the role of leadership in fostering participatory democracy, the role of leaders in policy-making and regeneration processes and the links between local leadership and economic development (Bussu and Bartels, 2014; Clark et al., 2015; Collinge and Gibney, 2010; Hemphill et al., 2006; Purdue, 2001; Vanderleeuw et al., 2011; Zhang and Feiock, 2010). The topic of what constitutes *effective* city leadership has been addressed in literature from scholars as well as private companies and multilateral organisations (Elcock, 2008; Hambleton and Sweeting, 2004; Hemphill et al., 2006; McKinsey & Company, 2013; PricewaterhouseCoopers LLP, 2005; Svara, 2003). In a review of the role of leadership in and for place Collinge et al. (2010: 367) have, for instance, flagged how 'effective leadership' is one of the main factors that explains how and why some localities 'are able to adapt to and exploit the opportunities afforded by the complex and rapidly changing social and economic circumstances of the modern world'. Yet often in the urban literature these types of assumptions remain unsystematic and the research underpinning them mostly anecdotal or place-specific.

What might be distinctive about city leadership, as opposed to leadership more generally, is its focus on place. In 'place-based' leadership processes, 'those exercising decision-making power have a concern for the communities living in a particular "place"' (Hambleton and Howard, 2013). Despite this important distinction, at the outset of this study we were particularly interested in identifying any work that applied prominent theories of leadership to the urban context. However, this search found few examples of this in research and practice. Today, the majority of the work on city leadership contains minimal if any engagement with leadership theories from other disciplines. When it does engage with this literature, it tends to be with a small sub-set of the rich and diverse field outlined above, such as individualistic theories (Hambleton and Howard, 2013) or managerial/hierarchical theories (Gibney et al., 2009). Work on city leadership often builds on this selective reading of leadership theory to highlight the supposed differences between places and organisations as entities to be led. A common argument is that general leadership theory focuses on the management of self-contained hierarchical organisations, where power and influence are distributed vertically, while city leadership involves complex networks of overlapping institutions (Beer and Clower, 2014; Collinge et al., 2010; Gibney et al., 2009).

Given the amount of literature on leadership, and the lack of clarity and consistency in defining precisely what 'leadership' is, it is not surprising that scholars of city leadership gloss over much of general leadership theory. This is, however, unfortunate because in recent years there appears to have been a distinct, if not yet universal, shift in orientation among scholars of leadership. As the review above demonstrates, many contemporary theories of leadership explicitly acknowledge that organisations work in an increasingly collaborative and networked fashion (Denis et al., 2001). Some contemporary leadership theories, in particular CLT, are designed specifically to grapple with complexity and there may be some value in scholars of city leadership building on these (Beer and Clower, 2014). In a recent book on place and leadership, D'Alessandro and Léautier (2016) have gone some way towards addressing this disconnect, seeking to 'stitch together' diverse theories of leadership and locate them in space (local, urban, regional and against other scales). They argue that it is fundamental to pay attention to the dynamics between leaders and spaces/territories. This is true, they suggest, for both theorists to 'place' leadership, and for leaders to 'know their spaces' well beyond the often marginal attention to the geographies of leadership.

There are of course some important differences between organisations and places. Place leadership is inherently political and requires a nuanced understanding of power (Hambleton and Howard, 2013). While leadership as a process of 'interpersonal influence' (Tannenbaum et al., 1961) invariably involves the exercise of power, this is something that, with few exceptions (e.g. Zaleznik, 1977) is rarely acknowledged in general leadership theory. Place leadership is dispersed across governance networks within which there are formal and informal leaders (Beer and Clower, 2014; Hambleton and Sweeting, 2004; Sotarauta, 2016). The involvement of informal leaders highlights another important point: leadership is not always a formal, paid role in communities (Beer and

Clower, 2014). Community leadership roles require people to donate time and resources. Thus, challenges to place leadership may include not just ineffective leadership but a lack of leadership – challenges that echo through this book from introduction to conclusion. To get to these challenges, however, we can build on the limited but potentially useful insights of the few theories of city leadership available today.

Theories of city leadership

City and place-based leadership research is a growing, but still small, area. Among the limited empirical work conducted to date, the majority are case studies of leadership processes or biographies of particular leaders (Beer and Clower, 2014; Gibney et al., 2009; Stone, 1995). Researchers of city leadership are not asking a consistent set of questions nor applying the same methods, which is limiting the generalisability of research in this area (Greasley and Stoker, 2009). Without a robust evidence base to draw on, the leadership of place is under-theorised (Gibney et al., 2009). A number of scholars have attempted to incorporate elements of some general leadership theories into their work. Purdue (2001) applied transformation / transactional leadership theory to a study of neighbourhood governance, while Beer and Clower argue for the value of CLT to the study of place leadership. Both Hambleton and Howard (2013) and Gibney et al. (2009) advocate a distributed approach to leadership in cities.

The theory most commonly mentioned in the literature on city leadership is facilitative leadership (Greasley and Stoker, 2008). Facilitative leadership has been a prominent theme in literature on leadership in education from the 1990s, where it has been described as similar to transformational leadership (Conley and Goldman, 1994; Guastello, 1995; Hord, 1992). Facilitative leadership is often used to describe the collaborative and collective approach taken by many elected urban leaders in North America and Europe (Greasley and Stoker, 2009). While formal political authority is exercised over others, facilitative leaders work with others, and 'serve' rather than 'steer' (Denhardt and Denhardt, 2003, cited in Bussu and Bartels, 2014). This approach can bring together people with disparate interests to work towards common objectives (Bussu and Bartels, 2014; Gains et al., 2007). Facilitative leadership is behind the collaborative behaviour seen in networked governance and partnership working; it brings together actors in complex and fragmented urban environments (Berg and Rao, 2005; Bussu and Bartels, 2014; Greasley and Stoker, 2009).

Facilitative leadership usefully integrates the study of city leadership with issues such as governance, politics, pluralism and participation. Greasley and Stoker (2009) link facilitative leadership to the process of forming urban governance regimes, while Svara (2003) suggests that adopting a facilitative style can help political leaders be successful in particular forms of urban government. Ultimately, however, facilitative leadership focuses on the leadership style of an individual, usually an elected political leader. Thus, while it emphasises that leadership is distributed and requires multiple actors, it is ultimately a theory about leaders rather than leadership.

This is a problem not just for scholars but for the city leaders and policy makers who wish to improve their practices. This problem is aggravated by a lack of conceptual clarity in the way we talk about leadership, such as the conflation of leaders and leadership. How we define and conceptualise leadership shapes our approach to making normative recommendations. Hence, to steer the direction of this project and its key findings, we found ourselves in need of a more applicable and methodologically systematic, but also clearer, 'theory' of city leadership – one that is 'generative' and sees leadership as a catalyst for action.

City leadership as catalyst: a 'practical theory'

A number of key observations about leadership stand out from our review of both the general and place-specific literature on leadership:

1. **Leadership is a process**. The majority of leadership theorists view leadership as an interactive process (e.g. Jago, 1982; Graen and Uhl-Bien, 1995; Bolden et al., 2003; Yukl, 1989). The process of leadership often leads to change, or creates something new (Asian Development Bank, 1999; Hambleton and Howard, 2013; Purdue, 2001; Verheul and Schaap, 2010).
2. **Leadership is distributed among many actors and institutions**. Leadership is not an individual activity, nor is it solely a government activity (Borraz and John, 2004; Palley, 2001). A range of actors and institutions are involved in city leadership.
3. **Leadership involves both individuals and the structures and institutions of local governance**. Individual leaders, while they play an important role, are only one element of leadership. The way in which local government structures and institutions are set up, the design of local decision-making processes, and the electoral

process all play a role in leadership (Elcock, 2008; Gibney et al., 2009; Grint, 2012; Hambleton and Sweeting, 2004; Hemphill et al., 2006; Howard and Sweeting, 2007; Svara, 2003).

4. **The process of leadership is complex and non-linear.** Leadership is more than the sum of its parts (Bolden, 2011; Gronn, 2000; Spillane, 2006). The interactions that occur in the process of leadership produce something new and distinct. The process of leadership can be complex and non-linear (Uhl-Bien et al., 2007).

Building on these, we propose here to take a broad view of city leadership as a composite of actors and structures, individuals and diffused systems, nodes and networks, which are assembled to drive action at the city scale. At its heart, we would argue that this assemblage view allows leadership to be understood as a catalyst for action. Building on the link between leadership and change, we propose that leadership can be understood as a catalytic process that brings together multiple elements of urban governance to identify and act on governance priorities. These elements fall into three categories: actors, structures and institutions, and tools (see Figure 2.2).

> ### Three elements of city leadership
> - **Actors** are the individuals and groups who often act as catalysts for interactions. They are those often considered to be 'leaders'.
> - **Structures and institutions** are the durable entities that establish and underpin the legitimacy of the actors and tools involved in city leadership.
> - **Tools** are the instruments used to action leadership. These are what actors and structures use to determine, codify and implement governance priorities.

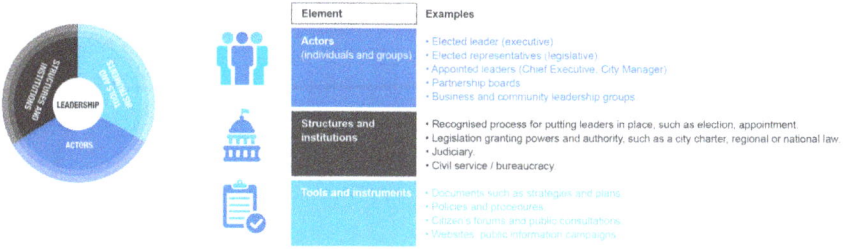

Figure 2.2 Elements of city leadership.
Source: authors

In chemistry, a catalyst, when added to a group of elements sets off a reaction between these, resulting in the creation of something new. Effective leadership is similarly transformative, bringing together the elements defined above in new ways that lead to new governance approaches, strategies and ways of working. Critically, in the process of leadership, these elements interact. Leadership is more than the sum of its parts. It is something greater that is created through interaction.

The process of leadership may operate in a number of ways. It may create something entirely new. It can also act to stabilise relationships between elements, leading to longer term, sustained initiatives. Leadership can also involve processes of altering or dissolving relationships when they are no longer working effectively. Examples of leadership, then, might include an appointed leader getting a partnership board involved in the development of a strategy, or a community group using its influence to encourage citizens to vote in an election. It could also be the decision to disband a partnership board.

Common to all of these processes is that they are not passive but, rather, the result of a conscious decision, by agents, to facilitate them. This reinforces the emphasis, found in much literature on leadership, on leaders, or 'agents' in the language used above. Leaders (or actors) play an important role in leadership processes. However, they do so in the context of structures influencing their operating environment and using tools at their disposal. We further explore each of the three elements of city leadership below.

The importance of the first two of these categories is clear from the literature. However, we would argue that the existing literature neglects the importance of the tools through which leadership processes are often carried out. Tools, such as plans, can provide a focal point for leadership processes and debates (Albrechts, 2004; Newman and Thornley, 2011). They may also be the main, material, tangible expression of leadership processes. For example, a strategy may be the main output of a lengthy debate about the best future direction for a city, and therefore a valuable way to gain insight into the processes, and outcomes, of city leadership. As the role of 'tools' as a defining element for city leadership has been least covered in the literature, we place a stronger focus in this book on understanding the shape and role of one example of a 'tool' for city leadership – the strategic urban plan.

Actors

A wide range of people are involved in city leadership both as individuals and as a part of groups. In cities, the highest profile individual leader is usually an elected mayor. However, other elected and appointed officials, private and third-sector actors and organisations often take strong roles in catalysing action and driving change in cities. For example, many cities have an appointed official, such as a Council Chief Executive or a City Manager, who plays an important role in city leadership. Most cities also have a legislative branch of government, as well as a range of other committees and boards tasked with particular governance responsibilities. Business and community leaders and organisations can also play an important role in city leadership. Citizens without a formal position in the structures of city leadership can also take on leadership roles through their involvement in community organisations or individual activism.

City leaders can come from many parts of society. What they tend to have in common is the capacity to mobilise people to pursue change (Heifetz, 1994) in the society and/or institutional settings within which they are embedded. Community-based organisations can be involved in city leadership, mobilising people and instigating change. The international NGO, Slum Dwellers International, supports women to set up and manage community saving groups. Women walk from home to home and gather small change from each household in order to collectively address the most vital needs of the settlement. This system of savings helps to articulate the community needs, represent it and negotiate change with local authorities but it also helps to fund upgrading projects pursued collectively. Individual actors within the public sector other than the mayor can also play impactful leadership roles. Recognising this, the 100 Resilient Cities project provided, for 100 successful city applicants, financial help and logistical guidance for establishing an innovative new position in city government, a Chief Resilience Officer, that would help advance the city's resilience-building strategies. Seeing leaders as one element of the broader assemblage that is leadership is, we argue, a fundamental step in developing an accurate and holistic view of city leadership. This perspective directs us to study not just leaders themselves but also the long-term trends, path-dependencies and levers available to these 'leaders' to catalyse action in their cities and beyond.

Structures and institutions

Structures and institutions are the entities that give leaders, and the tools they use, legitimacy. They are the relatively stable 'things' that enable and support the work of leaders. For example, political leaders such as mayors derive legitimacy, and hence the ability to lead, from acceptance of the system of election or appointment through which they obtained their position. Similarly, the power cities have to govern is usually granted through legislation passed by a higher tier of government (regional or national). The mandate of other actors involved in city leadership, such as partnership boards or local development corporations, is similarly derived from the institutions that establish them.

Leadership structures and institutions may be formal (required to be in place by a charter or law) or informal (lacking a statutory basis). Formalised leadership structures are often associated with a particular geography; for instance the boundaries of an urban area delineate where legislation passed by a city council applies. They can play an important role in ensuring the transparency, lines of accountability and stability of city leadership. Informal leadership structures, though they may lack the statutory basis of their formalised counterparts, can also play an important role in city leadership. The move from government to governance has led to the creation of important structures of leadership that sit partly or entirely outside city hall. These external structures that impact on city leadership are not just local. Increasingly, as we will argue, regional, national and international processes influence how cities are governed the world over.

An important characteristic of the structures and institutions of leadership is their durability. They tend to have lives far longer than an individual leader. They are not, however, immutable. Their existence depends on broad acceptance of their legitimacy and fitness for purpose. From 1993, New York City limited elected representatives to two four-year terms in office. In 2008, the City Council voted to amend the city charter to allow officials to serve three consecutive terms. This allowed then-mayor Bloomberg to successfully seek a third term in office.

Tools and instruments

Leaders can deploy a variety of different tools and instruments to set priorities, catalyse action or build coalitions (Albrechts, 2004). These include documents, such as legislation and policies, visions, strategies and plans. They may also be mechanisms for bringing together different people and groups, such as public forums and consultation groups. A city government may initiate the use of these tools themselves or they may be mandated to do so by legislation or another level of government.

Effective city leadership processes establish strategic priorities for a city. Plans are one tool that city leaders often use to do this, as well as to detail how these priorities and objectives will be achieved. Over the last 30 years, strategic planning has emerged as a popular approach to the planning process (Albrechts, 2004; Healey, 2007). Leadership tools like strategic plans play an important role in connecting leaders (people and groups) to the structures and institutions that allow them to catalyse action. As noted above, the connections they create are not just local but also reflect national and international factors that influence city leadership. For example, leadership visions may speak directly to, or borrow from, international frameworks like the Paris Agreement on Climate Change. Strategic plans as tools of leadership are the focus of chapter 5 of this book.

There are many different types of city leadership tools. With the development of information technology, innovative IT-based tools aiding city leadership continue to advance. Crowdsourcing web platforms are one such example. For instance, the mayor's office in Medellin (Columbia) launched MiMedellin, an open innovation platform where citizens can communicate with public authorities, either by voting options for existing issues, or directly proposing ideas. Successful tools can be replicated or scaled up to cover more than a city – a website/app called FixMyStreet covers the entire UK and enables anyone to report street potholes/bumps/problems with a postcode or through automatic geo-location. The report is then matched and sent directly to the council responsible.

Putting this approach to work

If leadership, as a process, is more than the sum of its parts, the elements of city leadership outlined above are obviously interdependent. Leadership is also not something that can simply be established. Rather it is a process of continual assembling and reassembling. Leadership in cities takes place through a diverse range of catalytic processes that bring together the agency of individuals and groups with the structures and tools that 'leaders' (and their constituencies) use to set and implement priorities. Some of these include council debates, public consultation events, plan and strategy development, and negotiations with other levels of government.

This conceptualisation of city leadership has implications for our understanding of what constitutes effective leadership. We will argue that effective city leadership requires bringing together all three of the types of elements described above. In addition, all these elements must be broadly accepted as legitimate and fit for purpose. For example, if the results of an election are questioned, the mandate of the elected leaders may not be accepted. If an influential group or demographic is not represented on a leadership body, its work may not be considered legitimate in the eyes of some.

In the analysis and discussion in the rest of this book, we will maintain a focus on leadership as a process involving each of these three interrelated elements. We will look at each element in turn but also explore how they interact and work together. Our aim is to demonstrate how analysing leadership as an assemblage of multiple interdependent elements produces both a robust analysis of leadership, and a pragmatic assessment of how city leadership can be better directed to address the many challenges facing cities today.

3
The shape of leadership: actors and structures

City leadership takes many forms. There are many types of leaders at the helm in cities, from populists and international personalities to entrenched bureaucrats and data-driven technocrats. Similarly, the structures that underpin city leadership vary. Whatever form it takes, city leadership, more than any other level of governance, is fundamentally about providing services to citizens. Due to their proximity to the populations they serve, city leaders are immediately accountable to their constituency. Despite this very local focus, at the same time cities are gaining recognition as potential agents of global governance. This is in part due to greater decentralisation, which gives cities more scope to operate on the international stage, but is also a result of the networking and lobbying efforts of city leaders seeking greater input into international governance discourse and global agenda setting. Effective city leadership and governance can impact not only local issues but also global affairs.

Central to our theory of city leadership is that individual leaders cannot be analysed and assessed divorced from their context. This context, at least for the scope of our review, consists of the institutions of local government and urban governance that underpin the capacity of leaders to address challenges, from everyday problems to complex global agendas. It also includes national and international dynamics, in particular the governance processes that take place outside of cities. It is therefore important, when researching city leadership, to consider leaders alongside and in interaction with the structures of local government, and influenced by broader political realities. This is particularly important given that currently, in many cities around the world, structures of local leadership and governance are changing. A trend towards decentralisation is leading to a wider recognition of the role of local authorities and an increase in their powers to act in cities (United Cities and

Local Governments; World Bank, 2009). Equally, as we highlighted in chapter 2, the shape and relevance of networking activities by cities (and their leaders) is also expanding as formalised 'city networks' grow in number and complexity. Managing and governing a complex urban environment presents a vast array of challenges for city leadership and governance. Not surprisingly, then, when respondents to our survey were asked to list the three greatest challenges facing their city, governance was the third most frequently mentioned challenge.

This is echoed in the work we have done ourselves with international urban initiatives. We asked members of the internationally-visible C40 Climate Leadership Group, a network of 96 among the world's largest urban areas, similar questions. Forty cities told us that governance challenges emanating from both local and national politics were among the most pressing problems for city leadership (C40 and Arup, 2015). As illustrated in Figure 3.1 overleaf, addressing governance challenges is a part of the activities of more than 40 per cent of all city networks today (Acuto, 2016) and is an issue debated extensively in international forums. These challenges are now of prime importance from all angles of politics, from local to national and international. We therefore begin this chapter by examining the structures that underpin city leadership, before moving on to looking at city leaders themselves. The chapter concludes with a closer look at the challenges that emerge from our global outlook.

Governance: assessing the 'structures' in leadership

Chapter 2 raised the debates around the issue of the appropriate scale for urban governance. In practice, urban government structures vary substantially both within and between countries. Governing cities is partly a matter of power. Yet decision-making and control are not necessarily distributed along clear and straightforward hierarchical lines. The research found that an array of governance arrangements of varying complexity exist around the world. At one end of the spectrum, in terms of complexity, are those rare 'city-states' such as Singapore, in which country and city are one and the same, that are governed by a single unified tier. At the other end, are federal countries such as the United States and Germany, where one or more additional levels of government exist between national and municipal government. The balance of power and responsibilities between levels of government varies from one nation to another, and even within nations. In Germany, for example, a small number of

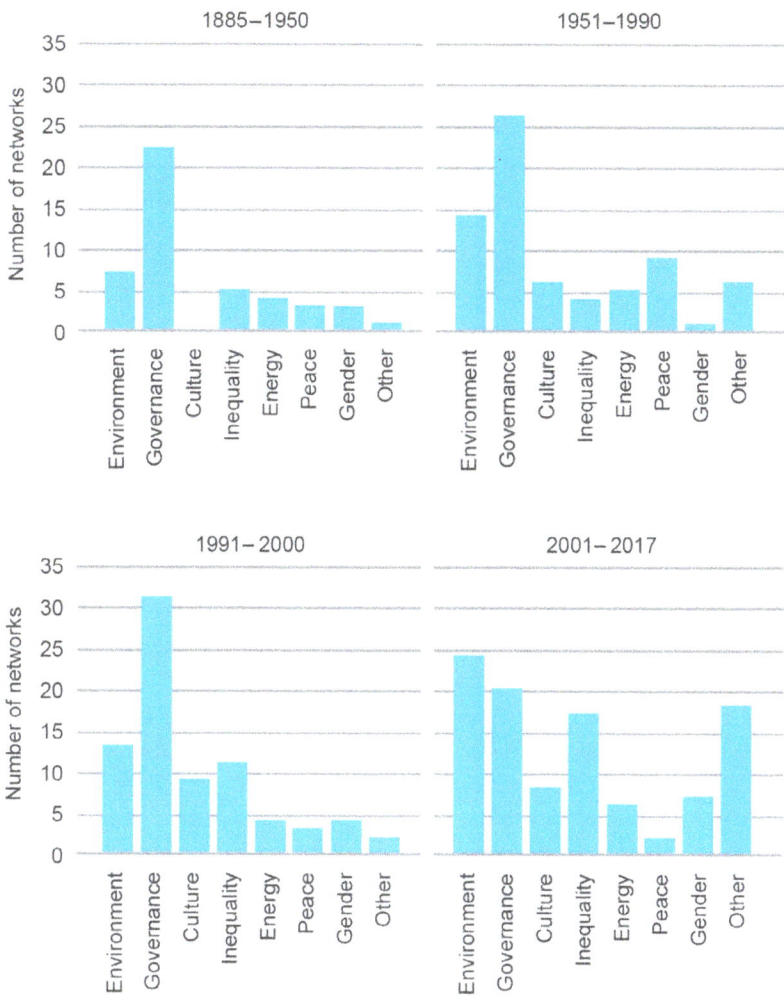

Figure 3.1 Key themes addressed by city networks per period.
Source: authors

cities, including Berlin and Hamburg, are designated as federal districts and hence have similar levels of autonomy to that granted to the Länder, or state governments, in other parts of the country. Similarly, Washington DC in the United States and Canberra in Australia are federal districts, though they have a more limited autonomy and influence at the national level. Cities also have varied levels of fiscal autonomy, that is, the level of freedom local government has to regulate and govern the taxation of businesses, residents and transient inhabitants (Slack and Côté, 2014).

In order to compare institutional models of urban government across the cities studied for this research, the team developed a basic typology of city government structures. Building on Goldsmith (2001) we distinguished between one-tier, two-tier and pluralised government structures. It is important to emphasise that the responses to the question about government structure highlight that 'city government' can be interpreted in various ways. Some respondents considered the city as an administrative unit, others took the wider city-region or metropolitan area as the basic administrative unit.

- *One-tier* **systems** identify cases where there is a single local government providing all services in a city or metropolitan area. Single-tier governance is more common in small cities and relatively rare in large metropolitan areas. Achieving this level of centralisation requires a process of annexation or consolidation and, in most countries, metropolitan areas are considered to be too large and complex for a single-tier of government to manage.
- In *two-tier* **systems**, the system of government structures is divided into nested scales. Typically, an upper-tier government structure takes responsibility for regional service provision and strategic planning across a large area, while a number of lower-tier governments deliver local services such as education and social services.
- In *pluralised* **systems,** the work of government is diffused across multiple authorities that have overlapping jurisdictions that do not neatly fit into a hierarchical government structure. The work of governing urban areas is shared between local government and entities created through voluntary or cooperative agreements between government jurisdictions.

For each city in the study, the research team identified the dominant government model, that is, the model that best describes the formal public sector government structure. In many cities, certain services may be managed through structures that differ from the dominant typology. For example, in cities with a one-tier government structure, pluralised arrangements may be in place to deliver a particular utility, service or governing mechanism, such as transport or energy systems.

It is important to highlight that this typology refers only to formal government structures, that is, it considers the existence of formal public sector organisations with specific governing responsibility for a city. The public sector is, of course, only one part of the network of organisations involved in urban governance. A range of other types of institutions, including partnership boards and voluntary groups, can also play a critical role in urban governance, contributing to both decision-making and service delivery. In this sense, whatever the formal government structure of a city is, the responsibility for agenda setting and decision-making of many cities is increasingly pluralised. Cooperative arrangements set out the relationship between different governmental entities (like local government authorities) and between these and private and non-profit partners. Sometimes, the different governing structures function parallel to one another without any clear set relationship – such is, for instance, the case in many cities where the city-wide public transport is run by informal networks.

Among the 202 cities studied, 63 per cent have a one-tier governance structure, making this the most common form. Thirty-four per cent of cities studied had a more complex government structure: 23 per cent of these had a two-tiered structure and 11 per cent had a pluralised structure. Several cities with particularly unique government arrangements fell into the 'other' category. These findings, along with expert responses about the effectiveness of each type of governance structure, are summarised in Figure 3.4 below.

Chapter 2 highlighted the recent increase in metropolitan-scale governance bodies. Our research found that, while single-tier government remains the most common form of city government, one-third of cities surveyed had a two-tiered or pluralised government structure. There was some variance in findings by region. Figure 3.2 summarises the breakdown of government structure by region. The majority of cities in Europe, North America, Latin America and the Caribbean, and the Middle East have one-tier government structures, while in East Asia the distribution is more balanced between one and two-tier structures. South and Central Asia has the most pluralised city governments, though this region also has one of the smallest sample sizes, meaning the figures may be somewhat less representative than those for other regions.

While the categories used above to classify local government structures are a convenient shorthand for understanding how cities are managed, there remains substantial diversity within each of the categories, particularly within the two-tiered and pluralised categories. Cities that respondents identified as having two-tier governments, for example, might have two tiers within the administrative unit or the wider region. For example, London's two tiers of government both exist within the formal boundaries of the city. Thirty-three local authorities in London are responsible for delivering a range of services, while the Greater London Authority oversees strategic functions. Neither tier's remit extends to the wider region of which London is a part. In contrast, Manila, in the Philippines, is one of a number of adjoining municipalities that make up

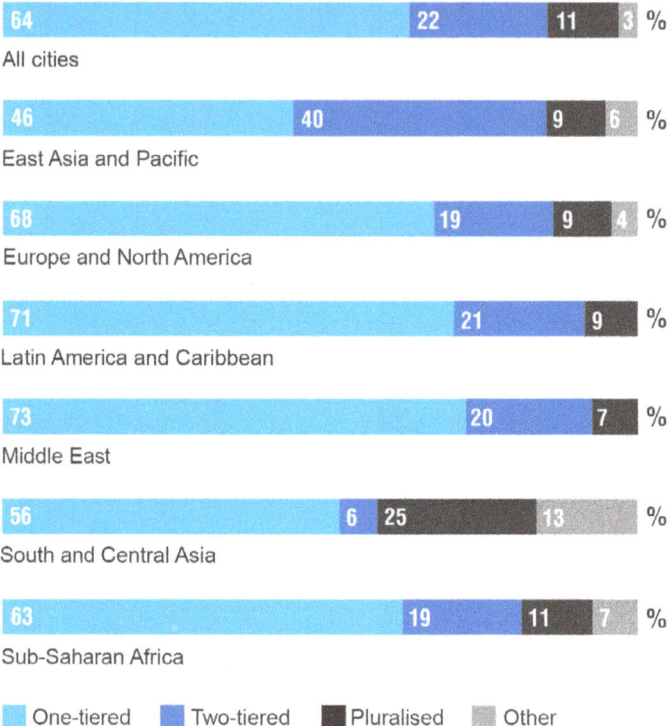

Figure 3.2 City government structures by region.
Source: authors

the Metro Manila region. Each city in Metro Manila has its own government. The Metro Manila Development Corporation (MMDC) coordinates certain regional functions.

A city's status in its national context does not appear to have a substantial impact on its government structure. Among those primary cities and capital cities classified by their national governments as states, rather than cities, government structures also vary. Washington DC in the United States has a single tier of government, while Berlin (Germany) has two tiers. Lagos (Nigeria) and Cairo (Egypt) have more complex, pluralised structures. Lagos is classified as a state and therefore has a governor, and 20 local governments with elected local chairmen, but no mayor. Cairo has no mayor and, instead, a governor appointed by central government is responsible for the city.

Equally, a city's participation in supra-national engagements does not appear to be directly linked to its underlying national status but highlights some important additional considerations related to the geography of city leadership (see Figure 3.3). Physically larger cities are part of

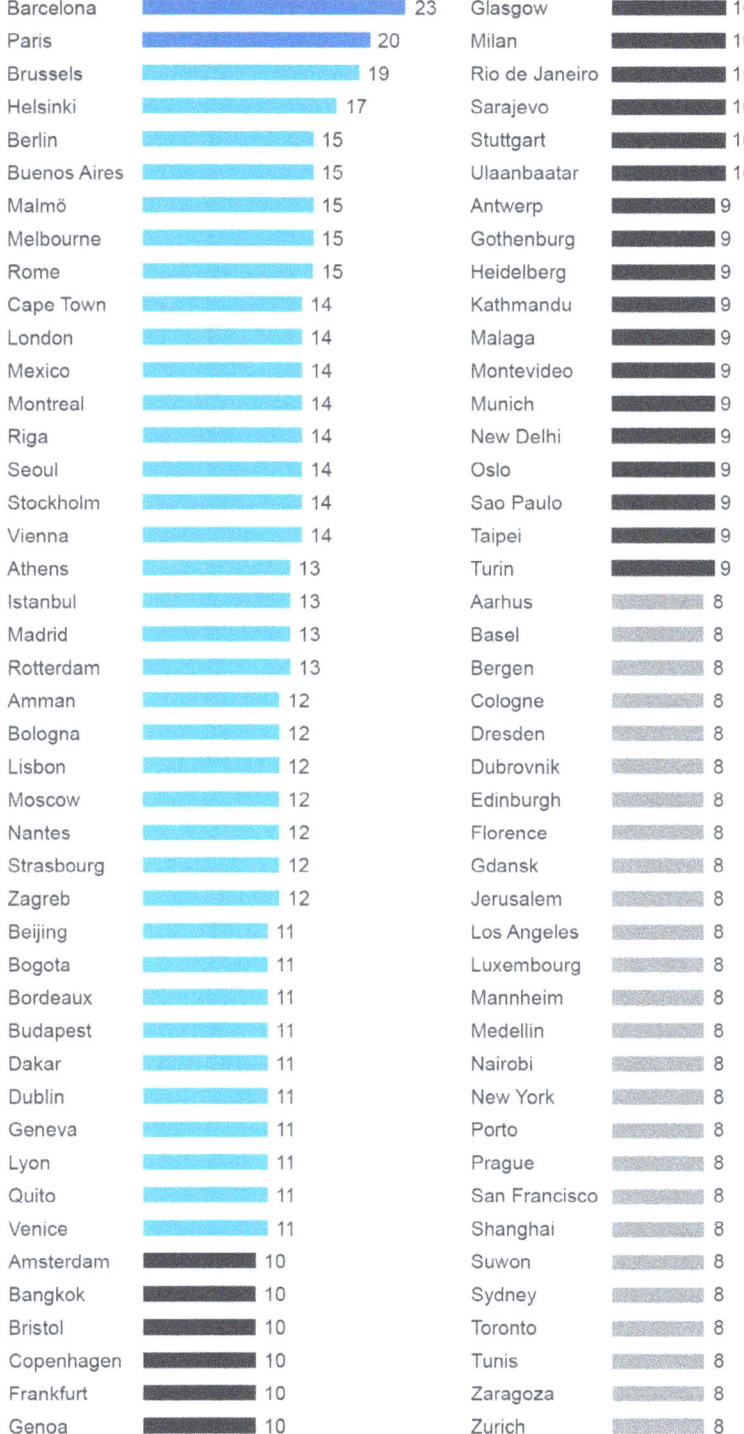

Figure 3.3 The 90 most networked cities by international city network membership.
Source: authors

more city networks than smaller cities. Barcelona is part of 23 (regional and international) city networks and plays a traditionally key role in facilitating the work of major international coalitions of cities like the United Cities and Local Government network (UCLG) and Metropolis. Paris follows closely with its participation in 20 city networks. This has brought the French capital into the international spotlight with its current mayor, Anne Hidalgo, playing an important role in the Paris Agreement summit in her capacity as the chair of C40 Cities. Brussels, Helsinki and Berlin are part of 19, 17 and 15 city networks respectively, showing that size is not everything in this context, and also confirming that, when we look at the whole list of highly-networked cities, tiered types of urban governance are not particularly relevant in determining which cities 'go abroad' the most.

Yet there remains some important Northern bias here: the only non-European cities in the top 10 are Buenos Aires (15 networks) and Cape Town (14 networks), and the majority of the most networked cities are European with just a few from the US. However, the 'top 90' of the world's most networked cities include a large representation of Global South cities. Once again there is no statistical correlation between governance tiers and size of network membership, which speaks to both the importance of reading governance structures in relation to the actors that populate them, as well as the growing internationalisation of city leadership in developing and developed contexts.

Government structure effectiveness

Government structure can have a substantial impact on the effectiveness of city leadership. To explore this issue, the *Urban Connections* survey asked experts to rank the effectiveness of their city's government structure in meeting the most important challenges facing the city over the next ten years. Overall, the largest group of survey respondents, 49 per cent, rated the government structure of their city as partly effective. Another 42 per cent of experts rated the government structure of their city poorly, that is, as insufficiently effective or not at all effective. However, this appears in a relatively different light if we break these down by type of structure (Figure 3.4).

More complex government structures may be seen as slightly more effective. Experts were slightly less likely to rate the effectiveness of two-tiered and pluralised government structures as insufficient or not at all effective. However, these differences are too narrow to make any

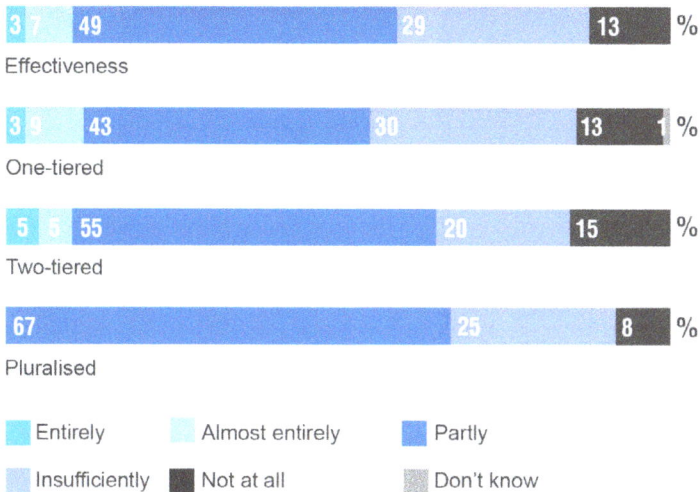

Figure 3.4 Government structures and their effectiveness.
Source: authors

conclusive statements. In addition, for a small number of cities, experts highlighted the connection between a one-tiered system and government effectiveness. In Dubai, the government is enabled to act upon major challenges as nearly all economic, planning and political instruments are centralised. Similarly, the centralisation in Panama City has enabled large-scale infrastructure projects (a new metro, bridge and highway) to move forward very quickly. Such top-down systems, however, are often not inclusive and do not consider the voices of the citizens, opposition or lower level bureaucrats. Future research could explore whether centralised governments can also be participatory, and whether there are city models that function successfully in that format.

This research has only begun to scratch the surface of the complex issue of government structure effectiveness. Our findings do point to two things. First, the overall perception, at least among the experts surveyed for this research, is largely negative. Experts do not see those who are putatively in charge of our cities as well equipped to lead. Second, this finding does not vary substantially between types of government structure. There is no 'ideal' government structure for maximising effectiveness.

Nevertheless, rapid urbanisation in many countries will lead to changes in government and administrative structures in cities around the world. Such changes can be complex and time consuming. At the same time, cities are also now increasingly acknowledged in international processes and debates. Issues of governance decentralisation to cities have been at the heart of the work of UCLG, a network of over one-thousand cities globally. Equally, cities have advocated for greater powers in a number of multilateral contexts, from the New Urban Agenda to the Paris Agreement on Climate Change. The 2015 United Nations Sendai Framework on disaster risk reduction even makes explicit reference to the importance of empowering local government to tackle international challenges such as those of natural hazards.

Several international scholars (e.g. Gordon and Johnson, 2017; Tavares, 2016; Khanna, 2016) have speculated that, as the number of international city initiatives grows and becomes more established in multilateral politics, pressure to enhance the political capacity of local governments in international processes will increase. If this occurs it will be a result of the work of both transnational city network initiatives, and the philanthropic and private sector organisations that are now increasingly used to collaborating directly with cities, bypassing national governments (Haselmayer, 2018). Given this, future research on the process of transition and the impact of changes to city government structure would be useful for city leaders. In addition, cities wishing to increase governance effectiveness may do better to focus on improvements to the more flexible concept of leadership, including how to build the capacity of leaders to effect meaningful change.

The leaders: assessing the 'actors' in leadership

To complement the data presented above, on the governance context in which leaders operate, the research for *Leading Cities* also gathered data on some of the key characteristics of the individual with the highest level of oversight in each city, usually a mayor. While our theory of city leadership goes beyond a focus on an individual 'leader' as the exclusive driver for change, the individual who holds the highest elected office in a city is the most visible embodiment of a city's leadership. Mayors tend to play a critical role in steering policy and practice in urban governance, catalysing action and change. They are closely associated with the successes of a city and held accountable for its failures. In addition, with the growing role of cities in international diplomacy, these leaders have greater visibility and influence on a global as well as a local stage. For these reasons, while we consider individual city leaders to be only one aspect of city leadership, examining who they are and how they come to be in a leadership position reveals a great deal about the current state of city leadership.

City leaders' gender

The research also gathered data on the gender of city leaders. Only 15 per cent of cities included in the research were led by women. A richer picture emerges when we examine the breakdown of these statistics by region. Latin American cities had the most balanced gender distribution, with female leaders representing 56 per cent of cities surveyed, that is 19 cities in total. The only region to have no female leaders is the Middle East. Figure 3.5 shows a full breakdown of leader gender by region. These findings raise a question as to what factors drive these regional differences. Further research might explore what has enabled women in Latin American cities to take on leadership roles at a much higher rate than in other regions.

Mandates of city leaders

Globally, 'mayor' is the most popular title for a city leader. Roughly three-quarters of cities included in the study had a mayor as did more than half the cities across all regions. The regions of Europe and North America, and Latin America and the Caribbean, had the highest percentage of mayors. After mayor, the next most frequent title was governor, which is usually held by the leader of the higher tier in two-tier government structures. It is also used in cities that are federal districts rather than normal municipalities. For example, the federal district of Brasília, the capital of Brazil, is considered a state rather than a city and is led by a directly elected governor.

The research team also identified the mandate of each leader, that is, how they were put into office. They may be elected, either directly by popular vote or indirectly, usually as the leader of the party holding the majority of seats in the city's legislative body. In other cases, a higher tier of government appoints a city leader. Figure 3.6 shows the percentage of cities with each type of mandate. The vast majority of city leaders (85 per cent) were elected. Among the cities using a process of appointing, responsibility for selecting a leader fell to a variety of bodies. For example, central governments appoint the mayors of Accra, Ghana and Minsk (Belarus), while the city council appoints the mayor of Ulaanbaatar (Mongolia). A small number of city leaders were neither elected nor appointed. For instance, the leader of Abu Dhabi, Sheikh Khalifa bin Zayed Al Nahyan inherited his position from his father. In Belfast, UK, leadership and governance structures are carefully designed to enable the city's leaders to manage the challenges of governing a divided city. A directly elected city council elects

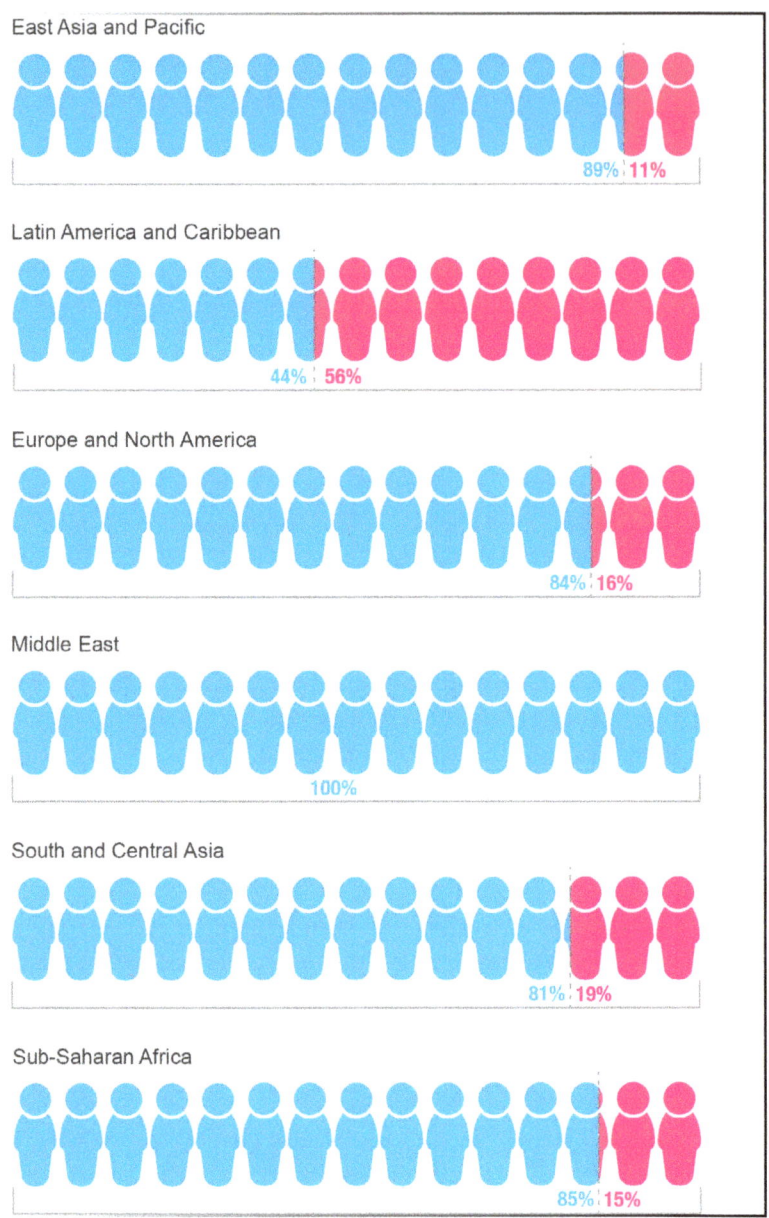

Figure 3.5 Leader's gender by region.
Source: authors

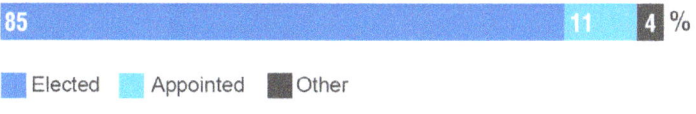

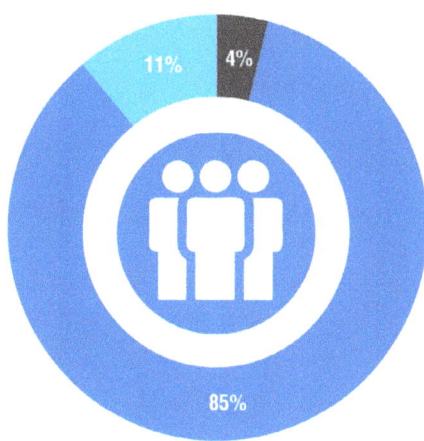

Figure 3.6 Leaders' mandate.
Source: authors

a Lord Mayor, who plays a largely ceremonial role and appoints a Chief Executive who is responsible for a range of leadership functions.

The research team also collected data on the length of time that the individual leader in office at the time of the survey had held his or her position. The overall average length of term was approximately four years. Regional averages differed minimally, with the highest average term length in the Middle East (5 years) and the lowest in South and Central Asia (3.2 years).

Building on this, the experts taking the survey were asked to rate the effectiveness of their city's government in addressing the city's challenges. Figure 3.7 presents expert respondents' views on government structure effectiveness broken down by the city leader's mandate. Once again, the data does not lead to a clear conclusion, though cities with elected leaders were more likely to be rated as having a government structure that was at least partly effective. Governments with appointed leaders were more likely to be rated as being 'not at all' or 'insufficiently' effective (47 per cent) versus 35 per cent for elected leaders.

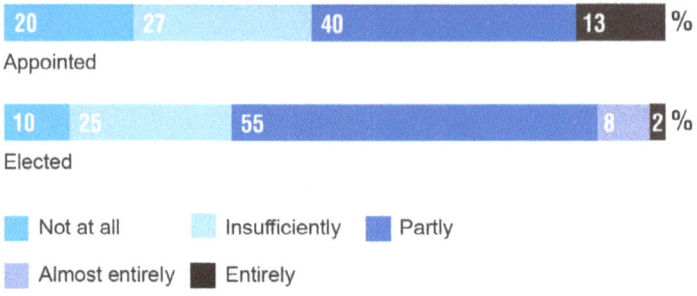

Figure 3.7 Leader effectiveness by mandate.
Source: authors

Emerging challenges between actors and structures

Formal and informal governance structures and arrangements shape the context in which city leaders operate. They are also, in our definition, a dimension of city leadership themselves, sitting alongside, and in constant interaction with, actors. The nature of these interactions can be what makes city leadership effective or not. A strong leader with a popular mandate can be constrained by an inefficient government structure. On the other hand, a government structure that works well in one city may not be able to overcome an inexperienced or unpopular leader who is unable to mobilise it to achieve his or her governing agenda. The importance of governance to effective city leadership came out strongly in the *Urban Connections* survey. Many of the experts who took the survey commented on the reason for their rating of government structure effectiveness. They were also asked about the main challenges facing their city and, in response, many of them focused on governance.

Analysing experts' survey responses on the topic of governance, we found that the three governance challenges that most commonly affect urban leadership and governance are: coordination between different sectors and tiers of government, financial constraints and corruption, and lack of participation and accountability.

Challenge 1: coordination between different sectors and tiers of government

The biggest urban governance challenge that emerged from the survey data is that of coordination between different tiers and different sectors of government. This includes coordination between different tiers and agencies in pluralised systems of governance, between the two tiers in two-tier cities, or between local and higher tiers such as state or national government. Urban governance is often shaped by national legislation and change is hampered by rigid or outdated national policies. In a survey response for Amsterdam, for example, our expert claimed that the financial problems and inequalities that might develop between cities were in part the result of a national policy to decentralise care for the elderly, disabled and youth. This highlights the role that urban leaders will play in tackling social issues, like catering for the needs of the elderly, that are not traditionally considered 'urban.' As populations age in many countries, urban leaders will increasingly be required to address the needs of older people. The World Health Organization has stated that 'making cities age-friendly is one of the most effective policy approaches to responding to demographic ageing' (World Health Organization). With social care funding often coming from higher tiers of government, but the demand for services concentrated in cities, there will be greater pressure on urban leaders to coordinate across sectors and tiers of government to effectively support vulnerable or marginalised groups of people.

The expert response for Seattle highlighted that policy is often set by the state legislature, which is not always responsive to the needs of cities. Changes to national and sub-national legislation are often complex and time consuming. This can make it difficult for cities to be nimble in their responses to emerging challenges. While cities have changed significantly in the past couple of decades, the 2016 State of World Cities report highlighted that most legal frameworks have remained very similar to what they were in 1996 (UN-Habitat, 2016b). Other cities struggle even to implement the legal framework currently in place – this is the case in Abuja, Nigeria where our expert noted that the city struggles to implement laws on environment, infrastructure and sustainability.

Recent decades have seen many countries give greater powers to lower tiers of government. However, the process of decentralisation is rarely smooth and in many cases brings its own, new governance challenges. This creates a whole new set of problems, where cities may be left in a vulnerable situation where they have decentralised political powers but incomplete fiscal decentralisation or a lack of capacity (UN-Habitat, 2016b). Many cities remain financially dependent on national governments. For example, the expert on the city of Bulawayo (Zimbabwe) commented that, while the local government administration is excellent, it is constrained by the lack of support from the federal government. This problem comes even more to the fore in countries where political conflicts are played out between city and national levels of government, such as in Caracas (Venezuela).

Another common problem that occurs within a city government is poor coordination and unclear lines of institutional jurisdiction. This is linked to the common practice of dividing up, by sector, governance activities and funds, with a number of agencies or departments each having a remit for a single issue, such as transport or the environment. In some cities, these individual agencies become siloed, leading to poor coordination and overlap of activities as well as duplication of efforts. In Bucharest (Romania) our expert attributed the inefficiency of government to the unclear delineation of responsibilities between city agencies. For instance, responsibility for environmental issues lies with the Bucharest Environmental Agency, Bucharest City Hall and a sub-department of the city government known as a Departmental Hall. The division of responsibilities between these institutions is not clear. Paris (France) was also flagged as an example of a city with a lack of government cohesion. The Paris expert noted that, for many, the many layers and authorities in the city government are confusing, and definitions of boundaries and decision-making responsibilities are disputed.

The majority of cities and metropolitan regions, or 66 per cent of those surveyed, have a two-tiered government structure. In some cities, there are two tiers covering the city itself. In others, a metropolitan tier goes beyond the administrative boundaries of a single city to cover the wider urban region. This latter approach, the creation of a metropolitan tier of government, has in many countries been a response to urban growth and territorial expansion, as many cities' administrative borders push further into surrounding rural areas, and municipalities merge and overlap. A strong argument for a metropolitan layer of government is its ability to drive greater efficiency and coordination. The respondent for Osaka, Japan noted that the ruling party has argued for consolidation between the region and its constituent cities, due to fragmentation and duplication of responsibilities across the Greater Osaka Metropolitan Area. However, the creation of an additional tier does not always remove fragmentation because the many independent municipalities constituting a metropolitan government may have local priorities that compete with those established at regional level. Our expert on Vancouver discussed this in relation to the issue of transport. Vancouver has a Metro Vancouver Board that brings together leaders of 24 municipalities. The city mayors pursue their cities' individual priorities, such as their desire to see rapid transit expanded in their jurisdictions, while the Metro Vancouver Board attempts to identify and pursue a regional approach. Another actor is also in the mix: TransLink, the regional transportation authority, is made up of officials appointed by the Province of British Columbia, who pursue a technocratic approach.

Coordination between tiers of government or, in contrast, a lack of coordination, also influences the participation of cities in the complex landscape of global urban governance discussed above. The wide literature on city networks and urban experimentation (Bulkeley and Castán Broto, 2013) demonstrates how local governments 'jump scales' rather than adjusting their governance structures, reaching out to peers, multilateral agencies and private actors 'abroad' to deliver strategic local initiatives. These practices can be empowering for city leadership but can also produce further challenges to coordination with other tiers of governance.

In many of the cases, city leaders have not just taken influential lobbying roles but also demonstrated a clear appetite to bypass their national executives (as seen in the stance taken by many US cities towards their federal government at the time of writing). Yet this implies in many instances a narrative of confrontation or substitution, rather than coordination, between tiers of governance. The argument of 'scale jumping' (Johnson, 2017) is centred on the assumption by city leaders that they have a 'strategic governance capacity' (Healey, 2002: 1779). Mayors have framed this capacity not solely in terms of international networking but also in terms of their deep reach into the everyday realities of their metropolises. Mayors and their peers have the responsibility for the daily management of most of the 'global' challenges recognised in the multilateral agendas (SDGs, Paris, Sendai) that define today's global urban governance. Former New York mayor and C40 chair, Michael Bloomberg (2015), uses the rhetoric of 'nations talk – cities act' and city leadership is 'the level of government closest to the majority of the world's people' as evidence that they are 'directly responsible' for the well-being and future of millions of urban dwellers. Whether this approach leads to positive outcomes or, in fact, further splintering of urban governance is a key question observers of city leadership should ponder in future research (and policy) agendas.

Challenge 2: financial constraints and corruption

The second most frequently mentioned challenge for urban governance in the survey was that of financial constraints and, relatedly, corruption and its impact on urban financial autonomy. For North America and Europe, financial constraints in cities in recent years are the result of austerity measures implemented after the 2008 financial crisis. Experts from a diverse array of cities, such as Beirut (Lebanon) and Bucharest (Romania) directly linked financial constraints to many of the challenges faced by their cities, from a lack of affordable housing to insufficient infrastructure or an inability to expand transport infrastructure. New York and Chicago in the USA, both cited financial constraints as a barrier to education funding. A vulnerable tax base was also mentioned by the experts on several cities in developed countries including Osaka (Japan), Luxembourg and Kansas City (USA), who noted that a vulnerable tax base could amplify their financial challenges in the coming years.

In the face of insufficient funding, cities in a number of countries have sought out foreign investment. Minsk (Belarus), for example, has received significant investments from China and the Middle East. Globally, foreign direct investment is rising, with 765 billion dollars being invested in developing economies in 2015 alone. Given this, cities may need to develop mechanisms to better facilitate foreign direct investments, as they may be crucial to the achievement of the SDGs. The United Nations Conference on Trade and Development (UNCTAD) predicts that achieving the SDGs by 2030 in developing countries alone would require an investment of between $3.3 and $4.5 trillion annually (United Nations Conference on Trade and Development, 2016).

Financial constraints were often very tightly linked to the issue of coordination between different tiers of governance and incomplete decentralisation. When discussing urban service provision and infrastructure, experts who took the survey frequently raised the advantages and disadvantages of a metropolitan tier of government. One benefit of integrated metropolitan governance is the economies of scale it offers for service provision, something that experts cited as helping overcome financial constraints. However, metropolitan government structures were not universally cited as having a positive impact on the finances of urban areas. In the metropolitan region of Lima (Peru), power is concentrated in the central metropolitan authority. Smaller municipalities have very little power or resources, making infrastructure and service provision quite difficult for them.

Greater decentralisation and devolution may also bring new challenges for urban governance. While increasing the power of local government is designed to bring government closer to the people, a number of experts pointed out that devolving power to local elites does not always result in the improvement of governance. In some cities, decentralisation may in fact represent a new opportunity for abuse of finances by government officials. In the *Urban Connections* survey, corruption and lack of transparency were cited repeatedly as important obstacles to effective governance and policy making. In Havana (Cuba), Rio de Janeiro (Brazil) and Minsk (Belarus), experts noted that there is very little transparency in how public resources are allocated. The political interests and political will of the administration was said to significantly influence public expenditure in cities of both developed and developing countries, such as Nairobi (Kenya), Valparaiso (Chile), Kumasi (Ghana) and Zurich (Switzerland).

This finding indicates that the problem of corruption deserves serious consideration in urban governance and city leadership, particularly when dealing with matters of finance. Corruption is one of the most pertinent and least talked about issues faced in urban governance. In an urban governance survey conducted by the London School of Economics, UN-Habitat and UCLG, the majority of city officials participating (65 per cent) rated the issue of corruption as not relevant or only somewhat relevant (LSE Cities, 2014). Yet more than 6 billion people globally live in a country with a serious corruption problem (Transparency International, 2016). Given this, it seems likely that corruption is quite common in urban government, a conclusion that the findings of the *Urban Connections* survey supports. Despite this, it has not been given a serious place in discussions on urban priorities at an international level; it has been called 'the elephant in the room in the New Urban Agenda' (Zinnbauer, 2016). Corruption was not covered in the World State of Cities Report 2016, it is only nominally mentioned in the New Urban Agenda and only one side-event was dedicated to the topic on Habitat III. It is a particularly complex issue, especially since, when it is rooted within governments, it is unlikely that those same governments will take steps to fight it, or to even acknowledge it as a problem.

Here the international dimension of city leadership, and the aspirations of global urban governance, are also performing poorly. If poverty, and to a lesser degree inequality, have been central themes of the emergence of a global focus on cities (Parnell, 2016; Revi, 2016), discussions as to the financial stability of cities have been sparse and debates on the problems of local corruption virtually non-existent. There is almost no international city network, for instance, which is geared towards tackling the issues of fraud and bribery within city leadership, and these debates tend to be relegated to a very marginal spot in favour of more pressing global agendas such as climate, resilience or health. Key international actors on this front remain for the most part in the non-governmental sphere, as is the case with Transparency International. They have only made timid moves towards efforts that, our experts tell us, are almost as central as the other challenges more commonly addressed by international urban initiatives.

Challenge 3: lack of citizen inclusion, participation and public accountability

Corruption often goes hand-in-hand with a poor record of civic engagement, the third most frequently cited governance challenge in our survey. It has been globally acknowledged that it is crucial for the urban governance and decision-making processes to be inclusive and to take a rights-based approach (UN-Habitat, 2016a). Inclusive planning and participation are a crucial tool for city leadership. It can offer direction and insight into how to ground decision-making in the local context rather than relying on foreign 'best practices', a common practice that has led to detached city development agendas and policies as they tend to disregard local circumstances (UN-Habitat, 2016b). Despite this, in many cities there are few opportunities for citizens and other stakeholders to engage in decision-making processes, or else participation opportunities are largely tokenistic.

The experts taking our survey flagged poor public participation as a problem in many cities across both developed and developing countries. In some cities, such as Riyadh (Saudi Arabia), Gaborone (Botswana) and Budapest (Hungary), experts reported that consultation and participatory planning exists only at a very superficial level if there is any at all. This typically means that there are consultation procedures in place but the wider audience is only given the choice to comment on already developed draft policies. In other words there is a limited opportunity to have a meaningful influence, or any real impact on the results by taking part in the process of their development. In more developed cities such as San Francisco (USA) and Stockholm (Sweden), experts framed the problem as one of 'political will', with big decisions open to only a narrow group leading to very ideologically limited debates. Another frequent observation was that decision-making processes are controlled by 'elites' in cities as diverse as Rio de Janeiro (Brazil), New York (USA) and Karachi (Pakistan). The impact has been that public investments serve limited groups: either those close to power or big developers.

These examples illustrate that citizen participation and accountability are crucial for successful urban governance, and therefore successful city leadership. It takes, however, all three 'elements' of city leadership to make this work. Having the right 'tools' and 'structures' in place, as is the case in Stockholm, where participation and public consultation are legally binding and enabled through a set of tools, does not suffice to guarantee a successful public participation process, without the 'political will' of the 'actors' that need to commit to just decision-making. Likewise, a strong city leader committed to inclusive planning would face a difficult challenge without the 'structures and institutions' that legally support a participatory process.

As meaningful participation takes place on a smaller scale, there is increasing pressure put on city leaders in local authorities to demand and enable public commitment 'to keep spaces for public consultation and planning open to the widest array of interests and opinion', ensuring the representation of a full diversity of interests (UN-Habitat, 2016a). Meaningful engagement should be strongly rooted in the context, practices and capacities of cities. It can range from a 20-person workshop with community groups when planning a slum upgrading project in Nairobi, to a 500,000-person nation-wide online survey when planning a large-scale infrastructure project in the UK. More and more avenues are opening up for inclusionary policies using IT tools, from online surveys, to e-governance systems and transparency and control mechanisms, to sharing publicly available information and enabling wide oversight.

Conclusions

This chapter has presented data on some of the fundamental aspects of city leadership for a large cohort of cities. While the cities included in the research vary substantially in size, culture and geography, there is some consistency in the way they are governed and led. Cities are likely to have a one-tier government structure and to be led by an elected mayor serving a limited term. Outside of Latin America, this individual is most likely to be a man. Leadership is likely to be hampered by the challenge of coordination as well as limited financial resources. When it comes to the structures of urban government, there are a variety of models but the survey found that single-tier governments were most prevalent. The data gathered on individual city leaders demonstrated a great deal of consistency across geographies and contexts, with the majority of cities having elected mayors serving terms of approximately four years.

Despite these consistencies, our findings indicate that there may not be simple, widely applicable solutions to the challenge of creating effective city leadership. For example, there was no clear correlation between the structure of city government and its perceived effectiveness.

Currently, the landscape of city leadership is shifting rapidly. In many parts of the world, urbanisation and urban expansion are more rapid than ever, while in others major demographic shifts are changing the types of demands to which cities need to respond. In this context, there is a great demand for solutions to the challenges of city leadership and governance. Cities are looking to their peers, international organisations, researchers and consultants for answers.

Solutions that focus on one of the three elements of city leadership, such as structures, but neglect the others, may lead to unexpected problems. This dynamic can be seen in the current trend, in many city-regions, to create metropolitan regions and corresponding governments. While these structures offer many advantages, it is important to remember that coordination and communication between different tiers of government was the most commonly mentioned obstacle to effective governance in our survey. Introducing new government structures may require putting in place tools to ensure that they work well with other structures of urban governance, as well as mechanisms to develop good working relationships between individuals that can help overcome the challenges of coordinating a multi-tiered urban government. This could be a simple tool, like a capacity building and skills development programme for the management and coordination of these processes, or a software ensuring data and information sharing.

Faced with limitations, as we noted above, many cities' leaders have sought to bypass the governance limitations of their urban and national governance systems and 'go abroad' to see more-than-local creative solutions. As noted in this and the previous chapter, the 'internationalisation' of city leadership is, however, not purely a bottom-up reaction. In the past few years, city leaders have had to deal increasingly with transnational concerns, such as migration or climate change, often with depleted financial, commercial and economic resources. Kearns and Paddison (2000: 845), for instance, have aptly pointed out how local governments are nowadays faced with three interrelated challenges: first, 'interurban competition has become fiercer' due to the heightened interconnectedness and pervasive territoriality of the global market; second, 'homogenising' global pulls are 'accompanied by simultaneous attempts to develop a city's local distinctive culture to attract business investment'; third, 'cities have viewed national governments as less able to help them and less relevant to their fortunes'.

Yet the internationalisation of city leadership, and mounting recognition in global frameworks, does not translate too easily into success. The majority of the experts consulted for this survey had significant reservations about the effectiveness of government and leadership in their city. Given this, there is an opportunity for further investigation into the role that city leadership can play in improving how cities are governed. The most commonly reported obstacles to effective urban governance in cities, were coordination between different tiers of government, financial constraints and corruption, and lack of participation. In addition to these, experts responding to the survey also highlighted the related challenges of the lack of capacity in many local government administrations, and the failure to be strategic and prioritise the most relevant issues in cities.

While these issues might seem obvious, they do not seem to have been given enough importance in international debates and multilateral agendas, and are therefore less likely to be sufficiently funded, or effectively targeted on a national and local level. For instance, as current as they are meant to be, the three-year-old SDGs are already not keeping up with some topics that have been emerging around and after Habitat III in Quito, particularly regarding these challenges for city leadership. For instance, the Quito Implementation Plan of the New Urban Agenda does dedicate an entire section to 'building the urban governance structure', but it is mostly general and vague, with the only reference to the changing landscape of governance structures being a commitment to 'promote a metropolitan governance that is inclusive and encompasses legal frameworks … '. The document does not give any specifics about where metropolitan governance is supported, and whether it advises transforming existing city governments or forming new ones. Nor does it detail what tools should be available to support these processes. This implementation gap has now been documented widely by scholars and practitioners alike (Simon et al., 2016), who cite both the complicated nature of putting into practice the aspirations of the New Urban Agenda and the monitoring required by the SDGs. The SDGs have been criticised for their unrealistic ambitions and vague instructions, focusing on targets rather than means to achieve these targets (Easterly, 2015; *Economist*, 2015).

In this sense, the role of city leadership in addressing challenges can go well beyond their strategic governance capacity and proximity to citizens. The catalytic role of city leadership also affords the possibility to link across often divided areas of international concern. While the inclusion of an explicitly 'urban' SDG (SDG number 11) is an important step, the urban dimension of other goals must also be taken up in implementation plans for the goals as a whole and could be catalysed much more effectively at the local level than, our experts tell us, is currently the case.

Two areas where our research demonstrates a clear need to think about the urban dimension of a broader goal are gender equality and finance. Our research found that women are poorly represented in the top tier of city leadership; only 15 per cent of the leaders in cities included in the survey were women. Goal 5 of the Sustainable Development Goals is to 'achieve gender equality and empower all women and girls'. One of the targets under this goal is to 'ensure women's full and effective participation and equal opportunities for leadership at all levels of decision-making'. To achieve this goal, we need to conduct further research on city leadership in Latin American countries, as this was the only region where a city was as likely to be led by a woman as by a man. Given that Latin America also has more female presidents than any other world region, it is important to examine what kind of lessons can be learned about female representation in leadership from this region.

Similarly, there are several finance targets under Goal 17 (partnerships for the goals), but they do not address city and urban governance specifically. In addition, most of the goals list targets and potential tasks for city leadership without acknowledging some of the main obstacles towards reaching these targets – namely insufficient funding and corruption on local and national levels. These are challenges that cities globally will struggle with as they work towards the objectives set out in the SDGs and the New Urban Agenda. The areas where governance has performed poorly can, in turn, be seen as potential focal points where a truly catalytic action by city leadership can make a difference. Changes in the shape of city leadership, and its focus on local, national or international challenges, or indeed a mixture of these, are important steps in the right direction. However, these also need to come with an assessment of the contextual structures city leaders operate in and, perhaps, bolder steps towards addressing gender inequality and corruption.

4
Setting priorities: local leadership in a global world

The diversity of issues debated in the run up to Habitat III, and at the event itself in October 2016, testified to the sheer quantity and variety of challenges confronting local governments. To respond to these, contemporary city leaders play many roles, from hands-on problem solver to international diplomat. Local government leaders must navigate the everyday challenges of service delivery, often with ever-diminishing resources. Alongside this, they also have to grapple with the impacts of new and rapidly evolving issues, from cybersecurity to a complex national and international political landscape. A typical day for a city leader might include addressing waste management in a specific neighbourhood of their city, and working together with other cities through networks like the ICLEI Local Government for Sustainability network and C40 to demand international action on climate change.

In this context, for city leaders it can be difficult to decide where to start and what to prioritise. Much of the work of leadership and governance is a continual process of identifying challenges and problems, establishing priorities and, ideally, transforming challenges into opportunities for progress. Therefore, in order to explore the current state of city leadership globally, the *Urban Connections* team sought to understand what are the most common types of challenges that city leaders face and to understand what actions they are taking to respond to them. In particular, we were interested in the scale at which issues are addressed and whether the issues cities focused on differed depending on factors such as city size or location. We also sought to identify common forms in which these challenges manifest and the ways in which city leadership is (or is not) attending to them. In this sense, we were also interested in the ways in which highly contextual problems can be reconciled with the developmental aspirations of leadership. In this chapter, we present an overview of the categories of challenges most frequently mentioned by survey respondents. The next chapter reviews how these are being addressed by city strategic plans as an example of a 'tool' that cities can use to map out their short- and long-term aspirations.

To help us identify key themes and priorities, respondents to the survey were asked to list, in rank order, the three most pressing challenges that their city will face in the next 10 years. The research team used content analysis to analyse the data set and identified the 10 challenges most frequently mentioned as affecting the 202 cities studied. These can be seen in Figure 4.1. While experts often responded to the

Figure 4.1 Challenges cities will face in the next 10 years, as identified by survey respondents.
Source: authors

question about city challenges with rich and contextualised descriptions of the challenges faced by their city, when the research team began to examine these a number of recurring issues emerged.

Below, we discuss the five areas most frequently mentioned as challenges by survey respondents. In doing so, our goal is to explore the ways in which governing structures confront these challenges, how they stand in between local and global pulls that define many of them and how city leaders practically respond or fail to respond to the difficulties of the contemporary urban condition. Some of the topic areas are inherently interrelated and have therefore been grouped together under broader categories in the discussion that follows. Table 4.1 summarises the five areas discussed below and the challenges respondents most frequently mentioned in relation to them.

While the precise issues reported by the experts were in many cases quite specific to their city, there was a great deal of thematic consistency, with cities large and small, rich and poor, North and South struggling

Table 4.1 Top categories of challenges cities will face, as discussed by survey respondents

Category	Topics
Mobility and urban connectivity	• Congestion • Insufficient public transit • Inequality of access • Poor planning and maintenance
Demographic change, poverty and social inequality	• Spatial segregation and unequal access to resources • Diversity and integration • Population growth • Aging population
Spatial planning and housing	• Lack of affordable housing • Urban sprawl • Informal settlements • Urban renewal and regeneration
Urban economies	• Economic restructuring • Economic diversification • Unemployment
Environmental sustainability	• Insufficient waste and sanitation management • Shortage of drinking water • Climate change-related risks, e.g. flooding and rising sea levels

with the same types of issues. Of course, many of the challenges reported, from crime to air quality, are both local and global in their causes and solutions. Addressing them is an inherently 'glocal' (Swyngedouw, 2004) affair. Solutions must be embedded in context but cities can also benefit from cooperation with their peers and engagement in international processes. What we are trying to convey here, then, is not a comprehensive ranking of issues for city leadership or to specify the causes of these issues, which vary from one city to the next. Rather, the following discussion offers an entry point into the menu of challenges that city leadership faces around the planet.

Of course, as the previous chapter demonstrated, leadership and its underlying structure is in itself a key challenge. The single most unifying theme in all the research findings was the challenge of effective governance. From the survey and the desktop research it became evident that the issue of effective governance is not only complex and wide-ranging, but also different in nature from the other challenges, as it deals with the obstacles that governments face when tackling these problems. We therefore decided to isolate this issue and elaborate the findings regarding effective governance outside this chapter. Chapter 3, and also chapter 5 on tools of governance (strategic planning in particular), are dedicated to this issue. Here our aim is to present and explore the operational side of city leadership at the local level by reviewing the issues that survey respondents said should be at the top of leadership agendas around the world.

Mobility and connectivity: beyond transport?

The capacity to connect people to jobs, services and markets, move goods and link ideas, cultures and service providers is critical to the vitality of cities around the world. Unsurprisingly then, mobility was the challenge that experts mentioned most frequently in the *Urban Connections* survey. It was also a common focus of the strategic urban plans surveyed by the Lab team. Within this category, congestion and infrastructure challenges were those most frequently flagged. These problems are common across all geographical regions, with East Asia and the Pacific taking a slight lead in the number of mentions.

Congestion and its impacts is an issue for a wide cross-section of the cities surveyed, from developed cities such as Sydney (Australia) and Munich (Germany) to regional centres including Maringá (Brazil), Kumasi (Ghana) and Port of Spain (Trinidad). This issue is well-recognised by both academia and central government. For instance, a report on urban mobility, sponsored by the US Department of Transportation, highlights the impacts of traffic congestion on liveability, affordability and greenhouse gas emissions (Schrank et al., 2011). In many developing countries, mobility and accessibility are declining as increased car demand and dependency lead to high levels of congestion (Schrank et al., 2011). In the survey responses, many city experts raised the issue of insufficient public transport infrastructure. This was attributed to a variety of problems, including a lack of funding in Vancouver (Canada), transport planning in Wellington (New Zealand), overdependence on private transport in Kuala Lumpur (Malaysia) and Xalapa (Mexico), and a lack of an integrated transit system in Amman, Jordan. The lack of equitable mobility was specifically flagged in smaller, second-tier cities such as Xalapa (Mexico). In many cities, certain groups have limited access to transportation as a result of underlying disadvantages arising from poverty, poor health or ethnicity.

Inequality in access to transport also emerged as an issue in a one-day focus group workshop, which the *Urban Connections* team held with urban experts and city officials in Toronto (Canada) in 2014. The Toronto city-region is experiencing a number of challenges resulting from 'bottlenecks' in its structures of connectivity. Systemic patterns of disconnectedness present long-term biases in transport and infrastructure investment. This then creates 'transit deserts', or areas poorly served by public transport. Congestion, created by employment and land-use patterns, as well as bottlenecks and choke points in infrastructure that cannot often be overcome (either because of large super-infrastructures shaping the whole conurbation or because of political-economic barriers), are a problem not just in Toronto but also in many other major international cities. The mobility of residents of Sydney (Australia), Kuala Lumpur (Malaysia), Dubai (UAE) or Hong Kong (China), also varies depending on whereabouts in the city they live.

In many cities, transport infrastructure is related to an overall dearth of effective physical planning, or indeed any physical planning at all. This is particularly the case in cities with limited financial resources, including Paramaribo (Suriname) and Port of Spain (Trinidad). In this light, many city leaders have prioritised the upgrading and maintenance of the physical infrastructure in their urban centres. Other respondents pointed to structural renewal and improved provisions of public amenities in Monrovia (Liberia) and Nicosia (Cyprus).

The question of mobility is tightly interwoven with the challenge of effective governance and, in particular, the shifts towards a city leadership that is conducted in partnership with non-governmental actors. When designing effective urban systems, the benefits and drawbacks of public and private modes of transportation need to be considered in decision-making: accessibility, affordability and convenience must be weighed alongside implications for financing and environmental impacts. As a way to optimise convenience (more typically associated with private transport) alongside cost and environmental impacts (more frequently benefits of public transport), a recent trend has occurred towards car- and bicycle-sharing schemes, particularly in Europe, North America and Australia.

However, research and feedback by experts has noted how the benefits of such schemes may be distributed unequally, with individuals and neighbourhoods that have a higher socioeconomic status gaining the greatest benefits (Ogilvie and Goodman, 2012; Ricci, 2015). These schemes may also neglect peripheral neighbourhoods. For example, in Tirana (Albania), periphery-centre access is considered a major problem that is not addressed by the initiatives focusing on the city's core.

Many cities have schemes in place to encourage active forms of transport, such as walking and cycling, and 'smart mobility' systems have been suggested as a way to increase pedestrian and bicycle route efficiency (Vishwanath et al., 2014). However, city leaders may not prioritise alternative options such as bike lanes, which several experts see as worryingly lacking in some cities.

Above all, the research findings demonstrate that mobility is often not an isolated technical problem but one that is interlinked with both social and environmental issues. City leadership should address the challenges of mobility and connectivity in an integrated, cross-sectorial manner. There are lessons to be learned from successful mobility projects, particularly with the rise of smart technologies and apps aiding city transport projects. City diplomacy could be of value for city leaders in this area, where city networks such as Polis or the Union Internationale des Transports Publics (UITP) advance development of mobility policies and knowledge exchange between cities.

Social change and inequality: leaders for *whom*?

Cities are diverse by nature; they attract a variety of businesses, people and cultures, generating infinite possibilities for social interaction. This brings many benefits, including economies of scale and opportunities for innovation. At the same time, research suggests that many social problems are amplified in urban centres. As the world's economic hubs, cities attract a range of skill-sets from the labour force. The concurrent demand for both very highly skilled and unskilled workers creates significant disparities in urban centres. UN-Habitat has regularly reported a trend wherein GINI Coefficients, which measure inequality rates, are often higher in cities than in national averages (López Moreno et al., 2015). In other words, in the majority of countries, city dwellers face higher inequalities than their rural counterparts. Importantly, this has increased over time. For example, researchers found a growing positive correlation between wage inequality and city size in the United States between 1979 and 2007 (Baum-Snow and Pavan, 2012).

Inequality can pose serious challenges for urban stability and cohesion. The challenge of creating and maintaining social harmony among a diverse, and often unequal, concentration of people emerged from the *Urban Connections* survey as one of the most important issues faced by city leaders globally. Cities in our survey that mentioned this challenge are both large and small and are located in both developing and developed countries. Social change and inequality are a global phenomenon. Cities around the world are deeply affected by problems of marginalisation, inequality and poverty. This raises a critical question for city leadership: for *whom* are cities led?

Though the challenges of inequality are manifested differently and to varying magnitudes between cities, a high proportion of our survey respondents (13 per cent) claimed that inequality was a primary source of social problems in their cities. The OECD has remarked that the social consequence of inequality 'is a multi-dimensional phenomenon requiring a multi-dimensional response' (OECD, 2014: 140–1). Social disparities in cities have spatial impacts, wherein economies of agglomeration incentivise 'various degrees of residential differentiation' (UN-Habitat, 2011), often leaving vulnerable populations cloistered in areas which offer little access to adequate infrastructure, basic services, jobs and social safety nets, and are often exposed to climate change-related risks and natural hazards.

The spatial dimension of social change in cities, then, becomes as critical as its economic and demographic dimensions. For instance, in Doha (Qatar) spatial segregation is a major challenge for city leadership and the growth of informal settlements discussed below is also a rising concern.

Social inequality manifests in a variety of ways. The affordability of housing (addressed later in this chapter) and food were frequently mentioned by survey respondents. Rising food prices globally, doubled with spatial segregation of populations, means that much of the world's urban poor struggle to afford and access adequate food supplies (UN-Habitat, 2011). This is reflected in the diversity of cities that specifically mentioned food inequality. These included relatively poor cities such as Bulawayo (Zimbabwe) and Antananarivo (Madagascar) but also cities in more affluent countries; Washington DC in the USA also suffers from food deserts according to our survey.

Social inequalities are also amplified by international and ethnic diversity in cities, with immigrants traditionally drawn into urban centres. At present, at least one-third of the population of many of the world's global cities, such as New York, Hong Kong, Los Angeles and London, are immigrants (Kemeny, 2013). Other cities have even higher rates of immigration, with extreme cases such as Dubai in the UAE (80 per cent immigrants) but also large and diverse metropolises like Toronto in Canada (51 per cent immigrants) or Brussels in Belgium, where 46 per cent of the population is of non-Belgian descent (Price and Benton-Short, 2007). These cities face the growth of ethnic enclaves and the challenges of social integration as different languages, religions and customs arrive and intermingle in close proximity.

In other cities, issues around integration are heightened by the intersection of diversity and the proximity to regional instabilities or civil war. Due to the rise of regional military conflicts, particularly in the Middle East and North Africa, an estimated 12.4 million people were newly displaced due to conflict or persecution in 2015 alone (out of a global total of 65 million refugees and displaced people) (UNHCR, 2016). Many of these displaced people end up in cities. Survey respondents for Tripoli (Libya) and Beirut (Lebanon) cited the influx of people from countries such as Syria and Palestine as challenges. Long-lived confrontations also impinge on the effects of social change and inequality, such as the disconnect between the Chinese and Malay populations in Kuala Lumpur. As diversity is disproportionately an urban phenomenon, city leaders will find themselves closely involved in determining how immigrant populations are to be integrated into society, in tackling discrimination and in ensuring equitable access to services and opportunities.

In addition to growing diversity, other aspects of demographic change were cited by survey recipients. Population growth was reported as a challenge in many cities, such as Kumasi (Ghana), Beirut (Lebanon) and Lyon (France). Other cities reported the hard-to-manage issue of overpopulation, including Astana (Kazakhstan), Bangkok (Thailand) and Malé (Maldives). Some cities are experiencing 'youth bulges', and struggle to integrate large numbers of young people into labour markets that are already largely saturated (KPMG, 2016). In other cities, a declining birth rate is contributing to a larger proportion of elderly people. Respondents in our survey that referenced elderly care and pension provision as major social challenges included a variety of cases such as Calgary (Canada), Changwon (South Korea) and Amsterdam (the Netherlands). In these places, city leaders are increasingly being asked to answer to the health and social stability concerns of a larger-than-ever proportion of elderly populations globally. Population growth and increased life expectancies around the world will likely continue to exaggerate existing inequalities if adequate intervention from city leaders is not pursued. Creating opportunities for the old and young to engage in urban life and gain dignity for creating their own livelihoods will continue to be important objectives for city leaders.

Planning and housing: managing urban change

Forty per cent of survey respondents mentioned spatial planning-related issues as one of the top three challenges in their city. Spatial planning challenges are somewhat unique in that they effectively cut across all the other challenges described in this chapter. The organisation and management of space and urban form affects and is affected by all of the other challenges discussed in this chapter and throughout this book.

Managing and directing the use of urban land is one of the central tasks of city leadership. This task will only become more critical in the coming years. Recent research has found that, while the world's urban population is expected to double in 43 years, the urban land cover will double in only 19 years (Angel et al., 2011). The management of urban land will have to be done with careful consideration for another, closely related issue – how to provide urban residents with an adequate supply of good quality affordable housing options. Twenty-three per cent of survey respondents mentioned a lack of affordable housing as a top challenge for their city.

While survey respondents mentioned spatial planning and affordable housing as separate issues, in this section we discuss them together in the light of an increasing awareness of the strong relationship between them. Recent research has drawn attention to the fact that problems with affordable housing and housing supply in many places have been linked to spatial planning and planning-system regulations and constraints (Gurran and Bramley, 2017). The tendency of local and national leadership to isolate housing and planning into separate policies and departments has been recognised as part of the problem, with emerging global strategies, such as the UN-Habitat 'Housing for All', proposing an integrated vision of housing within national urban development frameworks (UN-Habitat, 2016b). The 'urban' SDG also addresses urbanisation and housing under the common umbrella of sustainable, safe and resilient cities.

Increasing rates of urbanisation have already outpaced that of many cities' capacity to plan for urban growth. In fact, one of the most common problems for city leaders, according to our survey, is managing urban growth. Experts mentioned this topic as an issue in Adelaide (Australia), Kumasi (Ghana), Nairobi (Kenya), Portland (USA), Stockholm (Sweden), Tripoli (Lebanon) and Zanzibar City (Tanzania) among others. One of the most urgent tasks for city leadership is to effectively use urban planning to prepare for urban growth and plan for urban expansion (UN-Habitat, 2014). Survey respondents stressed the need for 'more effective planning in general terms' (Abu Dhabi (UAE)), which largely means developing 'effective planning means and tools' (Nicosia (Cyprus)) and developing the capacity to implement and enforce land management and planning (Caracas (Venezuela), Amman (Jordan)).

The challenges related to population growth discussed above aggravate, in many cities, challenges related to land distribution and management, with experts reporting on 'lack of free space' (Huancayo (Peru)) and 'unbalanced land use' (Baguio (Philippines)) as a result. The failure to predict and plan for urban expansion and for housing supply in an integrated manner has, in turn, been driving the growth of typically very dense and poorly serviced informal settlements. While housing accounts for more than 70 per cent of land use in most cities, it has not been central to national agendas over the past 20 years (UN-Habitat, 2015). With an increasing reliance on the private sector, there has been a global tendency to 'enable' middle-class formal home-ownership, while 'disabling' access to adequate and affordable housing for the urban poor (UN-Habitat, 2016a).

Affordable housing is not just a problem for poor slum dwellers. Indeed, housing affordability stands on its own as one of the leading global problems for city leadership according to our survey. A lack of affordable housing was cited as a challenge by survey respondents from 27 cities across all continents (including Amsterdam (the Netherlands), Bangkok (Thailand), Beirut (Lebanon), Dhaka (Bangladesh), Leuven (Belgium), Maputo (Mozambique), Maringá (Brazil), Quingdao (China), Rio de Janeiro (Brazil) and Seattle (USA)). In addition, as previously discussed, high living costs and poverty were mentioned as a key challenge by 28 per cent of respondents. Statistics have shown that high costs of living, particularly in metropolitan areas, mostly come down to high costs of housing (Florida, 2014).

Informal settlements in particular, as an extreme urban symptom of the lack of affordable housing, emerged as a common challenge for city leaders in less-developed countries. In our survey, respondents from cities in many countries, including Algiers (Algeria), Bangalore (India), Kumasi (Ghana), Jeddah (Saudi Arabia), Ibadan (Nigeria) and Delhi (India) cited informal settlements as a key challenge. Global and local efforts have been directed towards improving the living conditions in informal settlements, particularly since the UN's Millennium Development Goals (MDGs) created a target, in 2000, of improving the lives of 100 million of the world's slum dwellers. By 2014, 320 million people had gained access to more-durable or less-crowded housing and improved water or sanitation. While this surpassed the initial target, the population growth rates mean that the absolute number of informal settlement dwellers has risen to 880 million today, compared to the 792 million reported in 2000 (United Nations, 2015). Tackling this issue will require city leaders to coordinate with non-governmental actors, such as community-led organisations like Slum Dwellers International. City leaders have to step up to address informal settlements comprehensively and on a city-wide scale, including efforts to plan them in relation to the broader city economies, utilise innovative financing options and recognise the informal forms of livelihood and employment (UN-Habitat, 2016a).

Another common outcome of ineffective planning is urban sprawl, increasingly acknowledged globally as a problem for cities. Low-density development patterns are associated with higher infrastructure and service-provision costs, and have negative environmental impacts as well (Clark and Moir, 2015; Henshilwood and Cullinan, 2012). While sprawling urban development is particularly common in North America and Australia, experts on cities across all continents mentioned urban sprawl as a key challenge. Problems with managing sprawl were mentioned by survey respondents referring to Baku (Azerbaijan), Brussels (Belgium), Warsaw (Poland), Calgary (Canada), Maringá (Brazil), Melbourne (Australia) and Kisumu (Kenya) among others cities.

Experts commented on the need to 'transition towards a sustainable urban form' (Brisbane (Australia)) or to 'redefine the urban development model' (Milan (Italy)). City leaders have a suite of policy options to make these changes, including encouraging transit-oriented development and increased density. However, the conflicting interests of decision-makers (planners, developers and government officials), as well as the reluctance of the general public to accept policy changes that affect long-standing living patterns such as low-density housing, can limit the effectiveness of these changes (Downs, 2005).

A final spatial planning-related challenge cited by a large number of survey respondents was urban renewal/regeneration. The responsible regeneration of out-dated city centres was also reported as an imperative for respondents from Berlin (Germany), Busan (South Korea), Bologna (Italy) and Barcelona (Spain), while in Minsk (Belarus) the expert cited the need to renovate former industrial areas. These responses highlight the main purposes of urban regeneration: to revive and attract investment to a declining city centre, or to regenerate or repurpose land formerly used for industrial purposes. Urban renewal is also often linked to refreshing city branding and identity. Experts on Aberdeen (UK), Portland (USA) and Gaborone (Botswana) also all mentioned the need to focus on place making.

Sometimes the 'image of the city' is less linked to its form and historical significance and more to its current state, particularly in the light of recent natural or man-made disasters. For example, the expert on Christchurch (New Zealand) reported that, following a series of major earthquakes in 2010 and 2011, repairing not just the city itself but also its image was a major challenge. The task of renewal is particularly delicate in cities where leaders must maintain parts of the built environment that are socially and culturally significant. Respondents from Jerusalem (Israel), Florence (Italy) and Istanbul (Turkey) all cited the fiscal and social challenges of preserving valuable quarters of their historic cities.

Spatial planning-related issues present a complex array of challenges for city leaders. The need to plan the use of land and the provision of affordable housing in private-market led systems is emerging as one of the challenges that city leaders will need to address in coming years. However, effective urban planning, as we will discuss in the next chapter, can also be an important tool of city leadership precisely because it cuts across so many issues, from housing, to environmental quality, to preservation. Strategic planning, we will argue, can help leaders develop solutions that tackle the many challenges outlined in this chapter. The role of planning is discussed in the next chapter about strategic urban plans (SUPs) as a tool of city leadership.

Ensuring economic vitality

Cities are the economic powerhouses of the globe. While urban centres are home to half of the world's population, they generate more than 80 per cent of global GDP (Dobbs et al., 2011). Increasing urbanisation has coincided with a growth in global economic interconnectivity in the last half century. Global trade has increased fivefold since 1980, with cities playing a central role in this globalised economy (Papageorgiou, 2009). In this context, the economic performance of cities has an impact that is not just local, but also national and international.

An essential part of city leadership is steering and supporting the urban economy. Ensuring economic 'vitality' (a term that we prefer to prosperity and profit) is a cornerstone of city leadership and one that presents myriad challenges. The *Urban Connections* survey found that the economic issues that city leadership has to confront range from the challenge of managing public finances, to the question of how to modernise and diversify city economies.

Many of the experts responding to the *Urban Connections* survey reported that their city was struggling with the challenge of restructuring their economy to keep pace with the changes that have come from economic globalisation. For example, experts on Busan (South Korea) and Valencia (Spain) mentioned difficulties in overcoming the industrial decline in their cities. Similarly, respondents from Detroit (USA) remarked that the decline of the manufacturing industry and the city's subsequent bankruptcy has been their primary economic challenge.

The challenge of diversifying an economy in order to make it more resilient to change was also reported by a large number of cities. The cities of Yellowknife (Canada) and Perth (Australia) have challenges resulting from their traditional dependence on successful mineral industries. The expert on Macau (China), responded that its economy is too reliant on the gambling sector. Respondents for Taipei (Taiwan) and Florence (Italy) mentioned that the strength of their tourism industries has prevented them from properly diversifying their economies strategically towards more sustainable growth sectors.

National economic issues, and the role that a city takes within the national economy, are also linked to the economic challenges faced by many cities. Survey responses indicate that the capital cities of smaller countries carry much of the burden for national economic management. For example, the respondent on Luxembourg remarked on the struggles of managing the city's tax base, as a large portion of its labour comes from beyond the national border. Overcoming the problems of a high level of international debt was reported as a significant economic challenge in Kingston (Jamaica). Similarly, the struggles of managing urban development in one of the world's fastest growing national economies (World Bank, 2017) was reported as a municipal challenge for the respondent in Santo Domingo (Dominican Republic).

Unemployment is also a major economic challenge faced by many city leaders. Respondents for cities in both developed and developing economies cited this issue, including Addis Ababa (Ethiopia), Atlanta (USA), Turin (Italy), Bulawayo (Zimbabwe) and Port-au-Prince (Haiti). Not only does unemployment pose a major obstacle to social and economic stability, it also presents a challenge for the stability of a state's welfare system. Reduced income tax collection and increased demand for social services pose major challenges for city leaders. Though most municipal governments lack the mandate to control national tax rates and unemployment benefits, they are still held accountable for the issues these create for their local populations. Similarly, although labour market programmes are often national priorities, responses to these challenges call for relevant and informed local input, given that most labour markets are localised. Among the cities that cited job creation as a priority were cases such as New Orleans (USA) and Bucharest (Romania), which emphasised that disadvantaged youth are the most affected by the lack of job opportunities.

Environmental sustainability: a truly 'glocal' issue?

Cities are engines of social and economic development but also use resources and generate waste at a higher rate than rural areas, particularly as urban populations continue to grow and concentrate. The impacts of human activity on the natural environment are highly evident in cities. Issues such as pollution, congestion, waste, energy and resource use, sprawling urbanisation, informal settlements, overcrowding and sanitation all pose challenges for the urban environment. This was confirmed by the *Urban Connections* survey, where a substantial number of experts (22 per cent) listed environmental concerns as one of the most important issues facing city leadership over the next 10 years.

While many environmental problems are global in scope, the wheels of the international diplomatic processes designed to collectively address these issues move slowly. In the meantime, cities have asserted a growing role in tackling environmental challenges. This can be seen in the growth of city networks (such as ICLEI or the C40 Climate Leadership Group) that campaign for greater global public attention to be given to the importance and capacity of city leaders to tackle environmental challenges, as opposed to international environmental frameworks. Research conducted by the Lab team, both within *Urban Connections* but also more specifically on city networks, confirms that cities play a key role in addressing the challenge of global sustainability (Acuto and Rayner, 2016).

However, city leaders do not always choose, or have the capacity, to *prioritise* environmental problems. 'Failures of governance' and the inability to 'implement preventive measures to reduce environmental problems or their impacts' (Hardoy et al, 1992: 23) have been cited as a root cause of many urban environmental problems today. These failures were evident in *Urban Connections* survey responses. A lack of infrastructure provision was cited as the cause of insufficient waste and sanitation management in cities like Maputo (Mozambique) and Zanzibar (Tanzania). Yet, on the other hand, city leadership can be a powerful force for addressing environmental challenges when supported by effective urban governance. Cases of forward-looking environmental leadership included examples like Vancouver (Canada) with its 'Greenest City 2020' strategy or Stockholm (Sweden) and its 'The Walkable City' focus. Scandinavian cases like Stockholm or Copenhagen have emerged as prominent examples of environmentally focused urban planning, with sustainability as a key thread running through all aspects of planning.

A shortage of drinking water was the most widely flagged environmental issue in our survey, with instances occurring in cities across all regions. Survey respondents related this challenge not only to insufficient infrastructure and to pollution, but also to a lack of provision resulting from various issues including development pressures. South and Central Asia had the highest relative number of survey responses related to the environment, with 75 per cent of the respondents including at least one reference to environmental problems. Water pollution, especially from a lack of sanitation infrastructure, was reported as especially problematic in this region, as well as in Sub-Saharan Africa. Waste management was also frequently cited as an issue in these regions.

Experts on cities from a variety of geographic regions mentioned climate change-related issues as important challenges, although the term 'climate change' was mostly used in reference to cities in Europe and North America. The most frequently cited urban challenges posed by climate change were increased instances of flooding and rising sea levels. These were referenced across all regions aside from Sub-Saharan Africa (examples include Alexandria (Egypt), Bangkok (Thailand), Miami (USA) and Paramaribo (Suriname)).

There is a close relationship between many of the environmental challenges mentioned by survey respondents and those discussed above in the sections on social issues and urban planning. For some cities, respondents linked environmental problems with social problems. These included environmental impacts on health in New York (USA), and equity and environmental justice in Washington DC (USA). Environmental problems often have the greatest adverse effects on the poorest groups in cities. This is particularly the case in cities with poor and insufficient planning, where infrastructure and service provision do not extend across informal settlements. This is a problem for the majority of bigger cities in the Global South, such as Cape Town (South Africa), where a challenge for city leadership is that informal settlers lack access to basic public services including water and sanitation.

The sprawl and rapid urban growth discussed earlier in this chapter has important spill-over effects affecting the environment. Experts on rapidly growing cities in the Global South, including Huancayo (Peru), Amman (Jordan) and Islamabad (Pakistan) cited the reduction of green, open spaces and the loss of agricultural land as major challenges. Other cities are prioritising the environmental aspects of urban planning, such as the maintenance of green space, in the form of parks and tree-lined streets, along with the preservation of natural habitat and biodiversity. In cities such as Brisbane and Adelaide in Australia, Vancouver in Canada and Leuven in Belgium, sustainability and environmental protection have become strategic priorities.

Conclusions

The findings from the *Urban Connections* research on the challenges for city leadership highlight that, despite varied contexts, there is a great deal of consistency in the issues faced by cities around the world. Many of the challenges discussed above are confronting almost all cities regardless of their context. Of course, these matters are not new yet it does not mean that they are homogenous, or steady. While the categories of problems faced by city leadership may remain consistent, the nature of the challenges themselves, and the means to address them, have evolved. Some issues have become more urgent. For instance, the impacts of climate change on cities become more evident as the frequency of climate-related natural disasters increases. In other areas, new solutions have emerged, such as the recent explosion in bicycle and car-sharing schemes as a mobility solution in cities around the world.

Given this context, city leadership must keep up both with the development of issues on the ground in their cities, as well as with advancements in governance and leadership approaches. Leadership must also adopt a strategic and joined-up approach to tackling challenges because the issues, as discussed in this chapter, are all inevitably complex and intertwined with other concerns. Global agendas, like the Sustainable Development Goals, have made the case for taking an international approach to identifying some of the issues and priorities discussed here. But city leadership is still a fundamentally local and contextualised process. This raises a set of questions on the dialogue between the different governance contexts in which city leadership plays out. How is the dialogue between these global realities and the localised processes of planning and governing shaping the catalytic process of leadership? How do both the growth in international processes and debates on urban issues influence leadership and governance at a local level? What are the ways in which city leaders are seeking to make sense of this global-local dialogue and what are their priorities? Whether it is urban planning and affordable housing, or living costs and inequality, addressing urban challenges in an integrated and strategic manner will be one of the biggest challenges for city leaders. To explore how this is done, we turn our focus in the next chapter to the third element of city leadership: tools. We do this through a review of the role of strategic urban planning in city leadership.

5
Setting directions: leadership and strategic urban plans

In chapter 2 of the book we proposed a practical theory of city leadership that frames leadership as a catalytic process, bringing together multiple elements to identify and act on governance priorities. These elements include three categories: actors; structures and institutions; and tools. Much of the existing work on city leadership focuses on the first two categories. While actors, structures and institutions are quite durable elements of leadership, often established through legislation, tools are more flexible and open. Tools can vary both in format and in impact and can take a variety of shapes but, broadly, they are used to agree, codify and implement governance priorities. Tools of leadership offer a tangible example of the catalytic role of city leadership. Examples of tools include plans, policies, forums, consultations, online platforms and apps. All of these offer a chance for the actors and structures of leadership to come together to take action in their cities. This chapter focuses on the role that tools play in leadership processes. It examines how city leadership is translated into strategic interventions in cities and how these interventions address the types of challenges to effective leadership and governance discussed in the last two sections of the book.

To do so, we focus on one type of tool of city leadership – the strategic urban plan (SUP). Strategic plans are a popular tool for setting long-term priorities for cities (Albrechts et al., 2003; Albrechts, 2004; Healey, 2007). We chose to focus on strategic urban plans in part because SUPs are also one of the most easily identifiable and readily available expressions of city leadership. They are relatively straightforward to access, review and compare, making them a good focus for a large international study of this type. In addition, SUPs are a useful focus for this study because they are not subject-specific. They usually aim to consolidate a city's priorities, strategies and targets for a wide array of subject areas, such as housing, transport and economic development, into a single document. Moreover, what sets them apart from other smaller-scale tools that focus on specific topics or shorter-term outputs, is that the delivery of SUPs is a long-term task requiring joint efforts and coordination between a variety of actors, structures and institutions in a city.

We hypothesised that strategic plans are a commonly used tool in cities around the world, something that the *Urban Connections* survey confirmed. Strategic urban plans are used by cities around the world to establish leadership priorities and set out what a city and its leaders aim to achieve in a certain time span. They connect leaders to structures and institutions, and aim to catalyse action. The process of developing a SUP can bring actors together to set out governance priorities. The plans themselves, when complete and adopted by a city, set out an approach to achieve these priorities. In this way, the process of strategic planning and the resulting strategic plan document, as tools, complement the work of actors and institutions in the leadership of cities, and provide a platform for bridging silos and building coalitions.

To study the role of SUPs as tools of city leadership, we first reviewed literature on strategic urban planning in order to establish the origins and role of strategic planning in city leadership, exploring the existing debates around the concept, which then framed our deeper 'dive' into the challenges and trends that have emerged thus far in *Urban Connections*. We then conducted two different pieces of analysis. The first was a landscape review of strategic planning practices. Using a combination of surveys and desktop research, we were able to obtain data on strategic planning in 143 of the 202 cities studied for this research. The second piece of analysis was a more in-depth review of 29 strategic urban plans for 26 cities and metropolitan areas. This chapter presents our findings on how strategic plans are used as tools of city leadership in a diverse cross-section of cities around the world.

A key tool for city leadership

Strategic planning is an approach to setting and achieving objectives that originated in military planning, and was adopted by the private sector in the 1950s. It involves 'general policy and direction setting, situation assessments, strategic issue identification, strategy development, decision making, action, and evaluation' (Bryson and Roering, 1987: 14). In the 1970s and 80s, government leaders became interested in using strategic planning as a way to help plan for an uncertain future (Albrechts,

2004). Rather than a homogenous or prescriptive tool, strategic planning is 'a set of concepts, procedures and tools that may be used selectively for different purposes in different situations (Bryson, 2001, 2003, cited in Friedmann, 2004). Strategic planning focuses on decision-making and implementation, as well as monitoring the impact of implementation (Parnreiter, 2011). The strategic planning process that is commonly applied in business and organisation management often produces a suite of outputs that may include a vision, a set of objectives, an implementation plan, or a strategy for achieving the established objective, and an agreed process for monitoring and reviewing those objectives.

While strategic planning has a wide range of applications, the type of strategic planning that occurs in cities is often referred to as strategic *spatial* planning (Albrechts et al., 2003; Friedmann, 2004; Healey, 2007; Newman, 2008). Here, the word spatial comes from the fact that strategic planning is often a tool used by spatial planners, and strategic plans for cities often have a spatial dimension. Strategic planning in cities is usually used as an alternative to detailed land-use planning, and focuses on higher-level objective setting. Strategic plans set out priorities and principles, not detailed policy or spatial design (Albrechts, 2004, 2006; Mastop and Faludi, 1997; Newman and Thornley, 2011; UN-Habitat, 2009). Strategic plans for cities do, however, retain a focus on a specific place or geographical area (Albrechts, 2004; Newman and Thornley, 2011). The practice of applying strategic planning in the urban context has its roots in Europe but has spread to cities in Africa, Asia and Latin America (Carmona, 2009; Parnreiter, 2011; Steinberg, 2005; UN-Habitat, 2009).

While the practice of creating a SUP is relatively widespread, strategic urban planning is still a relatively recent concept. Few cities and few countries have established norms for the processes and tools of strategic urban planning (Steinberg, 2005) and approaches vary both within and between countries and regions. For the purposes of our research, we define strategic urban plans as city or region-wide strategic vision documents outlining the development trajectory of an urban area, with a focus on the priority areas in that context. This is intended to be a broad and inclusive definition, incorporating plans that cover both cities and metropolitan regions, and plans that retain elements of a more spatially-oriented approach. SUPs may vary in their level of detail but usually strike a balance between a high-level 'vision' setting out a city's aspirations, and detailed plans for implementing specific projects, policies or programmes. They are usually developed through a process that involves some degree of collaboration between the various actors involved in a city's leadership. This, combined with the authority of the institutions that produce them, give them legitimacy as statements of a city's visions, agendas and priorities.

Strategic planning is primarily a locally-driven process but other levels of government can also play a role. As scholars of the impact of multi-level governance on urban policy in Europe have noted, the European Union has shaped the way in which key issues are interpreted and acted upon (Bulkeley and Betsill, 2005; Marshall, 2004). As with the other dimensions of city leadership, other types of non-governmental international actors can influence strategic urban planning. International city networks, such as Eurocities in Europe and United Cities and Local Governments internationally, can also influence strategic urban planning processes. Forums that act as platforms for knowledge exchange between cities, or joint initiatives and research, may feed, usually indirectly, into strategic planning processes. City networks and their supporters may also intervene more directly, as is the case with the Rockefeller Foundation's 100 Resilient Cities programme. This philanthropic project has supported 100 cities to hire a Chief Resilience Officer and prepare a city resilience strategy.

Multilateral organisations such as the World Bank and UN-Habitat also play a role in the strategic planning of some cities, particularly in the Global South. For example, throughout the 1990s and 2000s, the Cities Alliance, a partnership focused on helping cities tackle poverty through grants and knowledge sharing, has supported dozens of cities to prepare City Development Strategies. Their approach included a guide that contains both recommendations on which themes to cover, and a methodology for developing a strategy (Cities Alliance, 2006).

As a process allowing for a focus in leadership priorities and orientation, strategic planning can lead to change (building and promoting a new agenda for a city) or increase the stability of governance (Healey, 2007). In this sense, strategic planning fits well within the complex, networked nature of contemporary urban governance. Drawing on the literature on strategic planning with the theory of city leadership adopted in this book, we argue that SUPs as tools of leadership can do several things.

1 – Coordinate actors and institutions

The strategic planning process can bring together the many different public, private and civil society actors and groups with a stake in a city, and encourage them to work together (Healey, 2007). The process can provide an arena for playing out conflicts between different interest groups who wish to influence urban politics, such as public agencies, international businesses or civil society groups (Newman and Thornley, 2011). Strategic planning can build links, both upwards with other levels of government, as well as laterally with other key actors involved in leading a city (Albrechts, 2004; Hambleton and Howard, 2013).

2 – Broaden participation in city leadership

Closely related to its coordinating role, strategic planning can make urban leadership and governance processes more inclusive and participative. The strategic planning process is often initiated by local government, but involves a range of actors from the public, private, educational and not-for-profit sectors (Albrechts, 2004, 2006; Carmona, 2009; Healey, 2007; Mastop and Faludi, 1997). It should adopt a participatory approach that takes the whole city into consideration, with particular attention paid to vulnerable, poor and marginalised groups (e.g. UN-Habitat, 2016b). In this way, strategic planning supports efforts 'to break away from the functional/sectoral organisation typical of many national and regional/local governments, and to widen governance relations to incorporate in new ways significant economic and local community stakeholders' (Albrechts et al., 2003: 114).

3 – Establish durable governance priorities

Strategic plans set out priorities for city leaders to pursue. Being strategic requires being selective, so SUPs commonly set out a limited number of objectives and priorities and focus on these (Albrechts, 2004, 2006; UN-Habitat, 2009). Plans should also be forward thinking, setting out a vision for the future development of the city capable of mobilising stakeholders to engage and invest (Albrechts, 2004, 2006; Cities Alliance, 2006). Plans can help cities prepare for a range of possible future scenarios (Cities Alliance, 2006). If the plan-making process involves a broad coalition of actors and institutions, SUPs may withstand changes in government, allowing them to address issues that may take longer than a political cycle to address. However, one of the main factors for the success of the strategic planning process is that it has the support of city leadership, as implementation depends on the political will of mayors and other local authorities (Steinberg, 2005; Cities Alliance, 2006).

4 – Focus attention on implementation

Its focus on priority issues makes strategic planning a good tool for integrating spatial, social, economic and environmental issues into strategic directions. In a context in which local government cannot simply steer development, strategic planning can focus the attention of the actors and institutions involved in leading a city on particular issues (Healey, 2007). Strategic planning is action and outcome-oriented, focusing on decisions, actions, results and implementation (Albrechts, 2004, 2006). Strategies should be connected to tasks and there should be a clear commitment to implement the strategies. There should also be a monitoring and evaluation plan in place to ensure that the strategies are followed. Strategic urban plans should direct investment towards priority areas and cost-effectively allocate resources to strategic areas (Cities Alliance, 2006). Clear role descriptions for planning and monitoring should be established and the plan management should be 'institutionalised' (Steinberg, 2005).

While SUPs are an opportunity to tackle the challenges set out in chapter 4 (poor participation, uncoordinated governance, insufficient funding) – they are not immune to them. They are required to be selective in what they address, focusing on a limited set of issues. The process by which these issues are selected, in particular who is involved and how, is of course deeply political (Healey, 2007). As with all planning documents developed by local or national governments, legitimacy of SUPs can also be an issue. Ideally, SUPs should be developed through an open and consultative process (giving them input-based legitimacy), while the plan itself and the objectives and priorities it sets should be widely accepted by stakeholders (giving it output-based legitimacy). However, in practice, this can be difficult to achieve. Even if plans are accepted as legitimate, this can quickly change. If legitimacy is not something that is gained and held, but rather a continuous process (Bénit-Gbaffou and Katsaura, 2014; Suchman, 1995), SUPs are likely to need regular revisions. There is also an inherent conflict between the long-term ambitions of many strategic plans (which, as we will demonstrate below, often look forward 10 years or more) and the short-term nature of the political cycle in many cities. Plans can lack longevity and are sometimes abandoned with a change in political leadership (UN-Habitat, 2009; Wu and Zhang, 2007). In addition, even if the legitimacy of strategic plans is well-established, their practical delivery is carried out by many structures and institutions, which creates potential for the inter-institutional conflicts and political agendas. This also means that it is not only the change of political leadership that poses a risk to the delivery of SUPs but also changes among the other actors and organisations involved in their delivery.

To a great extent then, strategic plans as a tool for city leadership are reliant on the actors and institutions of city leadership, which shape the quality and eventual effectiveness of the SUP that emerges. Studying SUPs and the way they are developed offers a window into the process of city leadership. However, there is currently very little international comparative work on strategic urban planning. That which does exist draws conclusions from practices in particular regions of the world (Healey, 2007; Steinberg, 2005). With this in mind, the *Urban Connections* project reviewed the international landscape of strategic planning in cities. Our objective was to, through our survey, learn more about the nature of strategic planning practices across the diverse range of cities included in the *Urban Connections* research project and how these are used as tools of city leadership.

The international landscape of SUPs

Strategic planning is a commonly used tool in cities around the world. Out of the 143 surveyed cities for which we obtained data on planning, a substantial majority (82 per cent) either had some form of SUP or were in the process of developing one (see Figure 5.1), while a percentage of cities don't currently have a SUP, but have had one previously.

There was also minimal variation in these findings between regions. South and Central Asia were slightly more likely to have a SUP in place. Sub-Saharan African cities were less likely to have a SUP in place but many cities were currently in the process of preparing one.

SUPs are varied in their style, focus and depth. Some plans closely followed the approach to strategic planning used by many businesses, in which leaders set out a vision, strategic objectives, actions and an approach to monitoring and evaluation. Others took on only some elements of this approach, with a stronger focus on the objectives but less on the implementation and evaluation. Some cities' plans resembled traditional land-use plans and elaborated a long list of objectives encompassing almost all thematic areas, while some focused on a set of priority themes. There were some regional trends in the type of plan and what it was called. In Africa and Southeast Asia, many cities still describe their strategic plans as a masterplan or development plan, or have in fact master plans that have evolved to become strategic plans – with the variations in vocabulary and legal frameworks in each city, it can be difficult

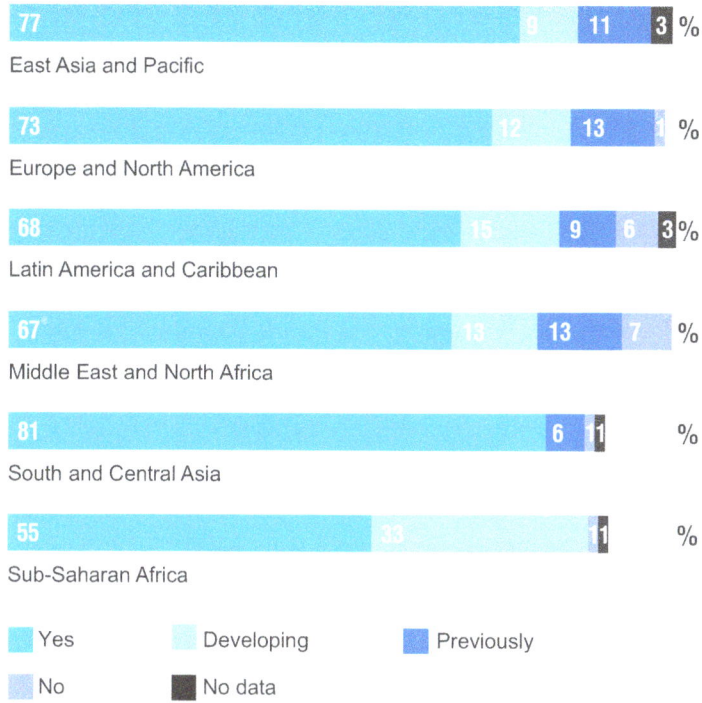

Figure 5.1 Status of SUPs by region.
Source: authors

to draw a firm defining line. In the other regions, SUPs were more likely to be called a city strategy, strategic plan or vision.

SUPs are also different in their temporal horizons. We considered this characteristic to be particularly relevant, as it speaks of the ability of these SUPs to deliver on one of the purported advantages of strategic planning for cities: a long-range vision (Albrechts, 2004, 2006; Cities Alliance, 2006). To evaluate plans' timeframes, we collected data on the start and end year of each plan and calculated the average duration of SUPs in the cities included in the survey that currently have a SUP. The average length of plans overall was 15 years, the median 14 years. The longest was Calgary's 100-year strategic plan. There was no significant correlation between the nature of a leader's mandate (appointed or elected) and the length of a city's SUP.

In the *Urban Connections* survey, we asked the respondents in cities that have a SUP to rate the effectiveness of that plan in tackling the major challenges facing the city and to comment in more detail on the reasons for the rating. Overall the response was more positive than that to a similar question about the effectiveness of a government structure. Seventy-one per cent of respondents replied that the plan was partly,

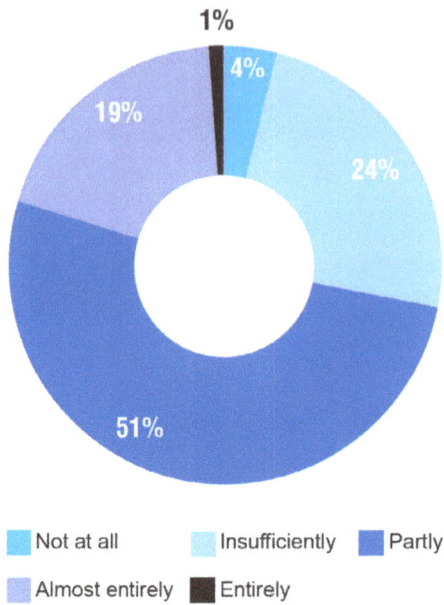

Figure 5.2 Strategic urban plan effectiveness.
Source: authors

almost entirely, or entirely effective, as compared with 58 per cent for the effectiveness of government structure (see Figure 5.2). This finding may imply that there is some degree of faith in the capacity of strategic planning or that it is perceived as a more articulated tool for city leadership.

We also examined the extent to which the objectives set out in SUPs were aligned to those challenges the expert for that city identified in the survey. Overall there was a great deal of overlap, with nearly all plans very or partially aligned with the key challenges for their city. This is of course only a very preliminary way to assess how well a plan addresses the challenges faced in a city, because it does not identify how comprehensively the challenges are discussed in a SUP or whether the issue is being addressed effectively. However, this analysis does indicate that SUPs do attempt to address some of the critical issues for their cities. In the next section, we take a more in-depth look at how strategic plans work in practice.

A tool for city leadership

To effectively analyse SUPs as a leadership tool required looking more deeply into the nature of strategic plans in a range of contexts. In order to obtain a representative picture of the strategic planning practice around the world, the diverse characteristics of strategic urban plans and their role in city leadership, the team reviewed the plans from 26 cities, which were selected to represent a cross-section of cities by region of the world, country, size and level of economic development.

The cities and plans examined are set out in Table 5.1. We attempted to gather an equal number of plans per region but this was not always possible as plans for some cities were not easily accessible. The majority of the plans selected address the city only. Some cities did not have a city-scale SUP but did have one for the metropolitan region. For three cities (Adelaide (Australia), Vancouver (Canada) and Manchester (UK)) there were both urban and metropolitan-scale plans available, as these

Table 5.1 Documents reviewed for this research

Region	City/Region	Country	Plan
East Asia and Pacific	Adelaide	Australia	City of Adelaide Strategic Plan 2012–2016; The 20-Year Plan for Greater Adelaide
	Hong Kong	China	Hong Kong: 2030 Planning Vision and Strategy
	Kuala Lumpur	Malaysia	Kuala Lumpur Structure Plan 2020
	Ulaanbaatar	Mongolia	Ulaanbaatar Master Plan 2020
	Christchurch	New Zealand	Urban Development Strategy
	Singapore	Singapore	Concept Plan 2011 and MND's Land Use Plan
Europe and North America	Vancouver	Canada	Greenest City 2020 Action Plan; Metro Vancouver 2040
	Stockholm	Sweden	Vision 2030: A Guide to the Future
	Zurich	Switzerland	Zurich Strategies 2025
	Aberdeen	UK	Aberdeen City and Shire Strategic Development Plan
	Manchester	UK	Manchester's Local Development Framework Stronger Together: Greater Manchester Strategy 2013
	Detroit	USA	Detroit Future City

Table 5.1 (Continued)

Region	City/Region	Country	Plan
Latin America and Caribbean	Rio de Janeiro	Brazil	Strategic Plan Rio de Janeiro Municipal Government 2013–2016
	Bogotá	Colombia	Development Plan 2012–2016
	Santo Domingo	Dominican Republic	City Hall Strategic Plan 2008–2015
	Port of Spain	Trinidad and Tobago	Sustainable Port of Spain Trinidad and Tobago Action Plan
	Caracas	Venezuela	Metropolitan Caracas Strategic Plan 2020
Middle East and North Africa	Cairo	Egypt	Strategic Development Plan for Greater Cairo Region 2050
	Tel Aviv	Israel	Strategic Plan for Tel Aviv Yafo
	Abu Dhabi	UAE	Plan Abu Dhabi 2030
South and Central Asia	Karachi	Pakistan	Karachi Strategic Development Plan 2020
	St Petersburg	Russia	Strategy for Socio-Economic Development for St Petersburg until 2030
Sub-Saharan Africa	Lagos	Nigeria	Lagos State Development Plan 2012–2025
	Kigali	Rwanda	Kigali Master Plan Report
	Johannesburg	South Africa	The Joburg 2040 Growth and Development Strategy
	Harare	Zimbabwe	City of Harare Strategic Plan 2012–2025

cities have both a city government and a metropolitan governance body. In these cases, the team analysed both plans. Table 5.1 lists the documents reviewed and the scale they address. The one outlier was Lagos, which is a state rather than a city. As the Lagos SUP is at the state level, it could be considered to be a metropolitan plan. However, there is some disagreement about whether the state boundaries encompass the metropolitan area.

The research team reviewed the data on SUPs gathered in the review of the plans above in order to explore if and how they support city leadership in the four ways identified from the literature review: establishing durable governance priorities, coordinating actors and institutions, broadening participation in city leadership and focusing attention on implementation.

Establishing durable governance priorities

SUPs can help consolidate longer-range visions for a city around which the citizens and different stakeholders can unite, setting the governance priorities and the path forward that the city leadership aims to set. These priorities are often articulated and summarised into vision statements and strategic objectives. Therefore, to analyse how truly 'strategic' SUPs were, the team checked each plan to see if it had a clear vision statement and set of strategic objectives. We then reviewed the topics covered by the objectives. Almost all plans (90 per cent) had vision statements and all of them had some form of strategic objectives.

The majority of SUPs reviewed were structured into strategic objectives, although these were referred to with different names throughout (themes, pillars, strategies, objectives). The 29 SUPs had between four and 20 objectives with themes that often converged. The most frequently covered theme was economic development, followed closely by environmental issues (see Figure 5.3). In some cases, these two objectives overlapped – for example, Vancouver's Greenest City 2020 Action Plan includes a strategic objective of achieving a 'green economy'. Other frequently mentioned topics were transport and mobility. The issue of liveability is addressed through the next three most frequently mentioned topics, all of which are related to quality of life: education, living environment and community needs.

SUPs should be tools of city leadership conceived broadly and not by individual political leaders. They should set longer-range agendas that transcend political cycles and bring together different political sides around a common vision. But how resistant to political change are SUPs? To test this, we evaluated whether SUPs can withstand a change in government. For the 29 plans selected for detailed analysis, we evaluated whether each plan had survived a change in government since 2000. A large percentage of these plans (45 per cent) had endured at least one change in executive leadership – that is, they were not withdrawn, changed or deemed invalid. In addition, changes in a SUP do not appear to be linked to a change in government. Some cities have planning cycles of a standard length. For example, Singapore's concept plan is reviewed every 10 years . While it appears that SUPs can often survive a change in leadership, it is more difficult to understand whether the change affected the extent to which the plan was implemented.

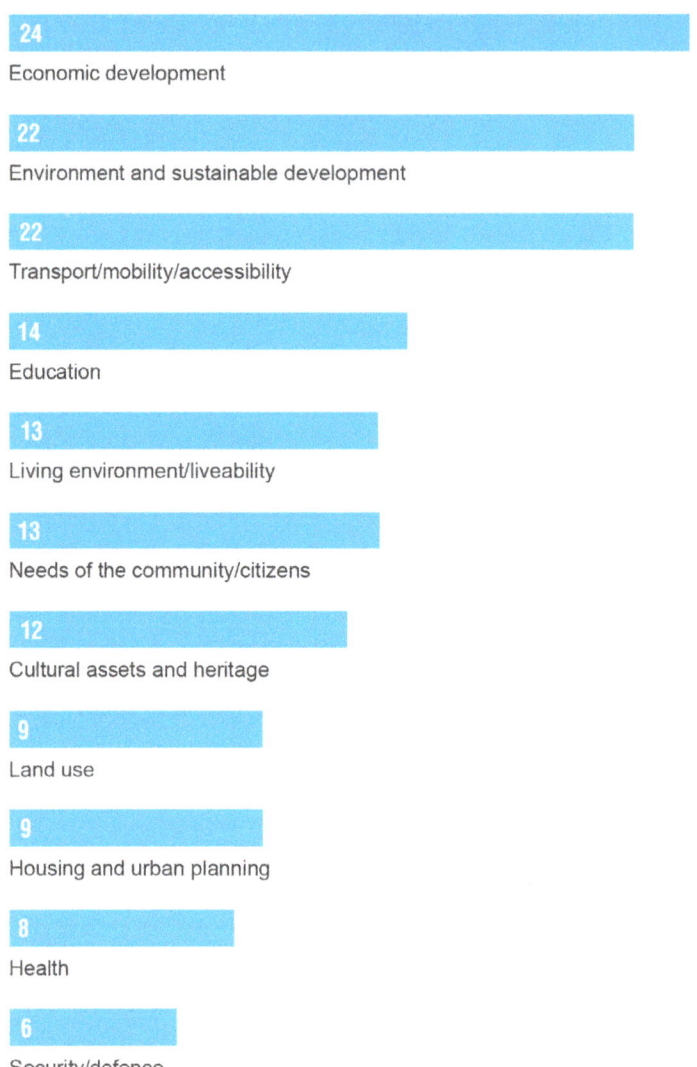

Figure 5.3 Most frequently mentioned themes in SUP objectives.
Source: authors

Coordinating actors and institutions

One of the most pressing challenges of urban governance is fragmentation or the poor level of coordination between the many different institutions and groups of people who play a role in cities. Our literature review pointed out that strategic urban plans have the potential to address this issue by uniting and consolidating these various players around a common agenda. This points to the importance of tools as a dimension of city leadership – they are the mechanism through which actors and structures are brought together to establish and work towards common goals. Leadership tools like SUPs can build links, both within different government sectors and between higher and lower government tiers as well as laterally with other actors involved in leading a city. For example, having a strategic plan at the metropolitan scale can help overcome fragmentation between local government jurisdictions and encourage a joined-up approach to managing urban change. To explore this coordinating role further, we reviewed plans for evidence of connections with other levels of government. While we cannot glean from the plan documents how collaborative the planning process was, we could investigate the links and references to higher tier plans and documents in the SUPs. Integrating a plan into existing higher tier plans suggests some level of communication and collaboration with actors in the higher tiers of government.

We began by simply looking for evidence in SUPs of intentions for the city to coordinate with higher tiers of government (e.g. regional, state, national). Most SUPs referred to other levels of government. Most of these had some evidence of coordination, meaning there were mentions of other levels of government (see Figure 5.4). For example, there are references to national strategies in the Kigali Master Plan Report but no details on how the plan aligns with these. The remaining plans were split evenly, meaning they identified other plans as well as how these plans aligned; for example, Hong Kong: 2030 Planning Vision and Strategy has a chapter on the national dimension of the plan but no evidence of coordination. An interesting focus for an in-depth case study of SUPs would be to analyse the levels of coordination and collaboration between actors and institutions in the – potentially decades long – practical delivery of strategic urban plans.

A SUP is rarely the only planning document in a city. In many cities, SUPs form part of a suite of plans. Often the SUP is the highest-level plan, with additional more sector-specific subsidiary plans and/or action plans sitting underneath it. SUPs can also be affected by higher tier plans, regional strategies, etc. In cities under the jurisdiction of a metropolitan tier of government, the city's plan may be positioned underneath or alongside a metropolitan plan. In some cases, national policy also establishes the context or environment in which a SUP is developed and operates. Relevant plans may also be developed by non-governmental actors.

Therefore, as another way to evaluate how strategic SUPs are in building links, the team also looked for evidence that SUPs linked to other plans or strategies – both links upwards to strategies and plans developed

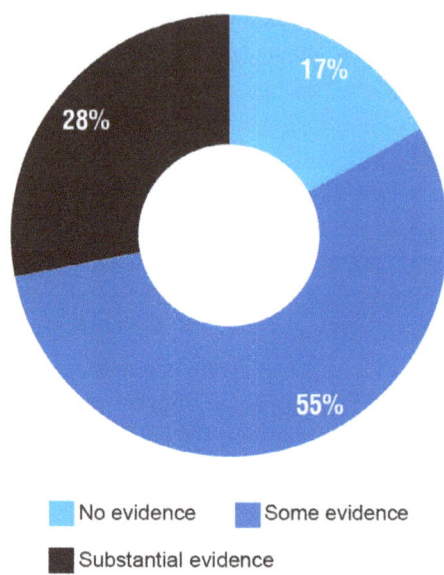

Figure 5.4 SUPs and evidence of coordination with other levels of government.
Source: authors

by higher levels of government (for example, if examining a city plan, then any regional or national plans) and links downwards (a plan for a particular topic, such as transport, or for a specific district of a city). The SUPs reviewed had very few links upwards (see Figure 5.5). Only three cities, Christchurch, Bogotá and Adelaide explicitly referenced plans and strategies from a higher level of government. By contrast, a substantial majority of plans (23 out of 29) referred to other plans or strategies being implemented from a city government level.

Finally, another relevant aspect of SUPs that determines their capacity as a tool to overcome fragmentation is how embedded they are in the system of structures and institutions, i.e. what is the legal format of strategic urban plans. Our research showed that while masterplans/land-use plans are commonly statutory, prescriptive and required by law, strategic plans are still more likely to be voluntary, i.e. not defined by legislation. Of our sample 29, 66 per cent were developed voluntarily, and 34 per cent were statutory. While a voluntary format has the advantage of deeming the SUP a more flexible tool that can be directed and adjusted by the local government actors, the potential drawback is that being outside of the structures, not backed up by any law or statute, it is often not clear how they are to be implemented, particularly when they are divergent from the existing statutory land-use plan. This lack

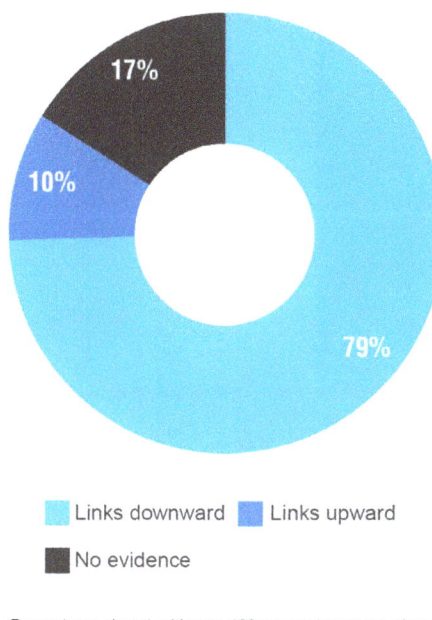

Percentages do not add up to 100 per cent as some plans had links both upward and downward.

Figure 5.5 SUP links to other plans.
Source: authors

of formal institutional approval and authority may limit the impact SUPs have as tools of leadership, and it would be interesting to further investigate how the balance between flexibility and innovation can be achieved for SUPs, and whether statutory support would help establish SUPs as stronger tools to counterbalance fragmentation.

Broadening participation in city leadership

One of the challenges of governance for local leadership found in the *Urban Connections* survey is participation and public accountability in the planning and decision-making processes. We hypothesised that SUPs are a tool that can contribute to broadening participation, because they should encompass a wide range of issues and provide an opportunity to give input in deciding which are the priorities that city leadership should focus on. The process of strategic planning is not straightforward to analyse and evaluate using a methodology in which the focus of inquiry was the end project of the planning process (the SUPs) rather than the process itself or the people involved in it. Accepting this limitation, we developed

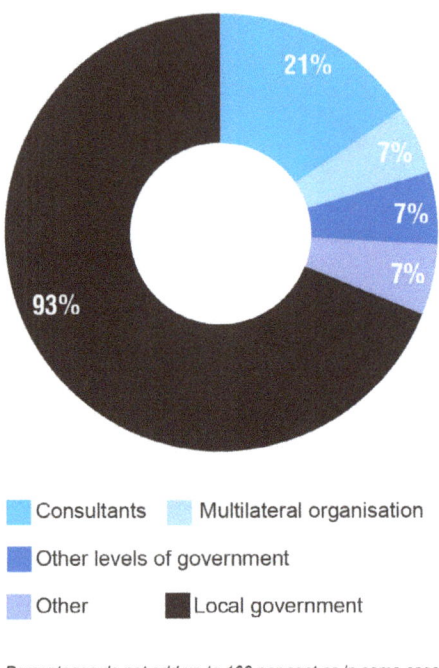

Percentages do not add up to 100 per cent as in some cases more than one organisation led the plan development process.

Figure 5.6 Organisations leading the plan development process.
Source: authors

a number of proxy indicators that could be used to give a baseline assessment of how participative the planning process was. We focused on who was involved in the process of strategic planning, as this information was either in the plans or fairly easy to obtain.

We began by identifying the primary organisations who initiated and drove the plan development process, leading on researching and writing the plan. Our findings indicate that strategic planning is a public-sector-led activity but involves a number of other partners. The vast majority of the plans (27, or 92 per cent) were driven by the relevant local government authority. However, in many cases, local governments worked with a partner organisation to develop their plans (see Figure 5.6). This was a mixture of consultants, multilateral organisations (such as the World Bank or UN-Habitat) and other levels of government. As can be seen in Figure 5.7, for the majority of plans at least one partner was included in the development process. These cases demonstrate how other levels of government and even international actors can play a role in shaping a SUP, making them more than just a local city leadership tool. While,

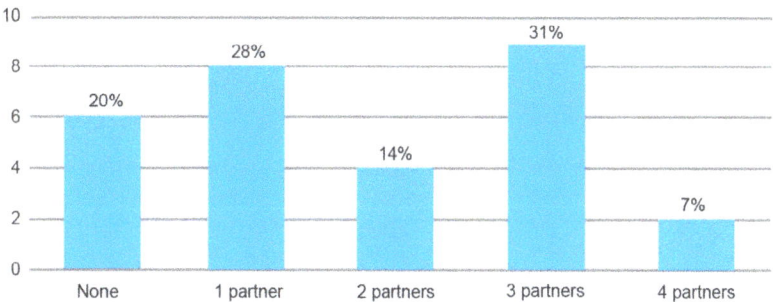

Figure 5.7 Partners in SUP processes.
Source: authors

overall, we found that all the SUPs we reviewed were largely focused on tackling local issues in the city they focused on, deeper analysis would doubtless reveal the way the agendas of these non-local actors shaped the tool that resulted.

We also reviewed the number and types of other organisations who, while not leading the process, were actively engaged and included in the development process through different participatory mechanisms. For 24 of the 29 plans reviewed there was evidence that other organisations participated in the plan development process. The most common development partners mentioned in plans were the local community and community groups, other levels of government and the private sector. The local community or community groups were listed as partners in strategic urban plans where community participation had a relevant role in the process. One such example is Bogotá's strategic plan for 2012–2016, titled 'Human Bogotá'. On its front page, the plan states that it is the product of a participatory process fostering direct democracy that consisted of around 300 meetings attended by 230,000 citizens.

Finally, we wished to understand how partner engagement actually fed through to the implementation of the plan. To study this, the research team reviewed whether the SUPs, in their action and implementation plans, mentioned projects and initiatives led by other actors involved in city leadership. The majority of SUPs (23, or 79 per cent) did do so. Most of the projects mentioned are being implemented by other levels of government, though some were led by the private sector as well. However, interestingly, even though community groups were the most common 'partner' in the process, the City of Adelaide Strategic Plan 2012–2016 was the only plan to include community-led projects. Adelaide, which promotes itself as having a strong sense of community, mentions activities such as a community events calendar, gardens, centres and clubs. It

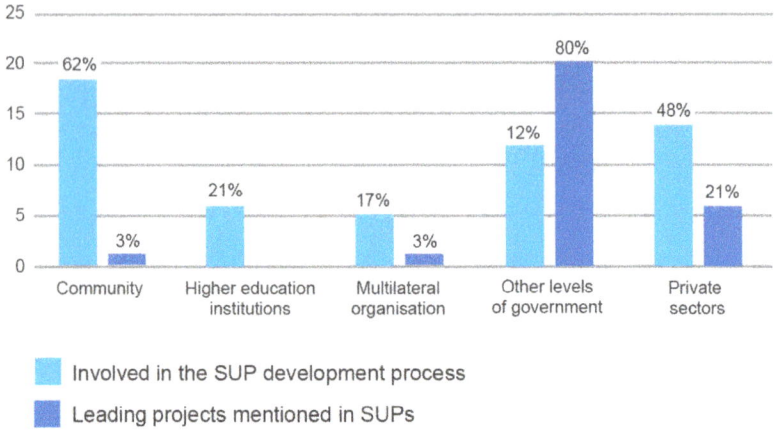

Percentages do not add up to 100 per cent as some plans involved more than one type of organisation in the plan development process

Figure 5.8 Organisations involved in the plan development process and project implementation.
Source: authors

appears that, in this sample of plans at least, involvement in the planning process does not automatically lead to direct involvement in the activities that emerge from the plan (see Figure 5.8).

This exploration of different aspects of participation in the process of strategic urban planning provides only a limited glance at the issue. To be truly effective as tools of leadership, SUPs would ideally be developed through a broad, transparent, inclusive process, adjusted to each context and circumstance – something that is best assessed through detailed case study research.

Focusing attention on implementation

To be true tools of city leadership, SUPs should do more than set out priorities for directing action and investment. However, the majority of plans – 66 per cent – were voluntary, meaning there was no statutory, legally binding imperative to implement them. The research team therefore looked for evidence of implementation plans or mechanisms that a city could use to take action on the objectives in the plan.

For the majority of plans, 72 per cent, there was substantial evidence of some form of an implementation plan; either a description of specific policies and mechanisms, or clear links to who would carry out actions included in the plan. For another 17 per cent of plans, there was only some evidence that an implementation plan was in place. These plans referenced implementation policies or implementing bodies but without detailed explanation, at times referring to additional documents that still needed to be developed. Approaches to implementation planning vary. In some cases, cities created new documents setting out how to take action on strategic plan objectives. Other cities aligned the strategic plan with other existing documents, plans and policies. Some plans were specific about who was responsible for taking actions, others left things more open.

The final element of SUPs that the research team analysed was their adaptability. Conditions in cities can change rapidly and city leadership needs to adapt and evolve. With an average length of 15 years, SUPs risk becoming out of date very quickly. Regular monitoring and evaluation (M&E) can mitigate this. For the majority of SUPs (72 per cent) we found some evidence or substantial evidence of M&E taking place, indicating that this important element of strategic planning has been embraced by many cities. Some plans specifically recognise the role of M&E in maintaining the flexibility and adaptability of the plan. For example, the Aberdeen City and Shire Strategic Development Plan identifies monitoring methods for each objective. It states that, even though the plan is to be revised every four years, monitoring must be continuous in order to ensure that the objectives are met considering the significant changes in society, economy, environment and population that will inevitably take place.

Our findings on implementation simply reinforce the strength of evidence that some form of implementation or M&E mechanisms existed. We recognise that successfully implementing a plan is far more complex than putting something on paper, and studying it requires more comprehensive research examining everything from coordination of roles and responsibilities within government, to financing mechanisms and competent staff. However, this initial desktop review does indicate that cities that develop strategic plans understand the importance of translating the plan into an action plan and monitoring it over time. Ultimately, however, the power of SUPs as city leadership tools depends largely on how they are embedded into the functioning of actors, structures and institutions.

Conclusions

The importance of strategic planning as a key driver to delivering successful urban development has echoed loudly across the statements of Habitat III and the UN's Sustainable Development Goals. While this research demonstrates that strategic planning is a popular tool in a wide range of cities, this review of the plans, their development processes and implementation, reveals substantial variations – in the plans themselves as well as in the process by which they are developed and implemented. Cities clearly see value in connecting this tool with other elements of city leadership. In almost all the plans we reviewed, while the city government led the planning process they included at least one development partner, and often more. The same is true for implementation, with many plans attempting to link the strategy to existing actors and institutions. Reviewing strategic plans in this way reveals the interrelatedness of the three elements of city leadership. It also demonstrates that the value of strategic planning as a tool may be in large part its ability to bring together many actors and institutions to work towards mutually agreed objectives.

A next step that could be of great use to city leadership would be to measure and evaluate the impact of strategic urban plans, and identify where SUPs have aided city leaders to advance their agendas and achieve positive change. This monitoring function is likely to be even more critical as other elements of city leadership evolve. For example, the number of newly formed metropolitan governments seems to be growing, reshaping the institutional landscape of city leadership.

While the pervasiveness of SUPs demonstrates that strategic urban planning is globally considered to be an important tool for city leadership, this is not visibly acknowledged on an international scale. For instance, strategic urban plans are not mentioned in recent multilateral agreements, such as the Sustainable Development Goals or the New Urban Agenda, and are rarely the object of international initiatives. The Quito Implementation Plan for the New Urban Agenda makes a series of commitments towards an 'urban paradigm shift grounded in the integrated and indivisible dimension of sustainable development: social, economic, and environmental'. However, it does not provide any specific planning instruments for implementation but rather generally mentions 'urban policies, strategies and plans', encouraging UN agencies, stakeholders and member states to 'generate evidence-based and practical guidance' for implementation. Strategic urban plans might be one such example of a planning instrument worthy of further exploration as a city leadership tool that could assist cities towards the implementation of the New Urban Agenda. However, their potential and effectiveness should be studied based on case-studies of current and past strategic urban plans, alongside other alternative city leadership tools.

6
Conclusion: a search for better city leadership

As city leaders begin to take a greater role on the national and international stage, so too should the practice and study of city leadership. This book has attempted to contribute to this emerging field by mapping the current landscape of leadership in cities around the world. Our approach was grounded in two principles: first, that studies of city leadership must go beyond a focus on individual leaders and, second, that they must take into account the experiences of all types of cities. Drawing on a study of leadership in a diverse array of over 200 cities, we have presented both a theoretical approach to unpacking and analysing city leadership and a broad evidence base about what it currently looks like around the world. We hope that this study will inform future work, by both scholars and practitioners, to better understand and improve city leadership practices around the globe.

Leadership, not leaders

In this book, we have argued that it is time to expand the definition of city leadership beyond individual leaders. Leaders are, without question, central to city leadership. However, a blinkered focus on individuals when studying city leadership risks overlooking the broader assemblage of multiple and interconnected elements that shape the way the process of leadership operates in cities. Effective leadership is not just something created by an individual. City leadership includes not just the efforts of visionary individuals but the structures and plans that are essential to turning an individual's vision into reality.

Therefore, we have suggested widening the focus of inquiry when considering how cities are led by thinking about *leadership* of cities, not just leaders. Building on data from a large sample of cities, we have attempted to demonstrate the value, for urban policy and politics, of an approach to studying leadership that considers the actors, structures and tools that form city leadership. All cities face leadership challenges, and studying leadership as a multi-faceted concept helps reveal them more quickly than looking at leaders alone.

In chapter 3 we reviewed the current characteristics of the actors and governance structures that formally make up city leadership in over 200 cities around the world. The overall perception of the experts who contributed to this research was largely negative. Leaders and structures, they noted, face significant challenges including coordination, finance and lack of engagement and accountability. The review of an important tool of city leadership, strategic urban plans, in chapter 5, allowed us to explore how cities are tackling both these challenges and the thematic challenges described in chapter 4. The process of leadership plays out through the development and implementation of these plans, whereby objectives and priorities are established.

One size does not fit all

Our research found that there is no template, model or one-size-fits-all approach to city leadership. Centralised, one-tiered, forms of urban governance were the most common system in the cities we studied. In addition, the cities did commonly have certain features, such as having a mayor, and some form of a strategic urban plan. However, there were no clear patterns or categories based on the type of city being studied. For example, it was not the case that widely known 'global' cities such as London and Tokyo took one approach and smaller cities, such as Nicosia or Recife, another.

In addition, as discussed in chapter 3, there are also no evident correlations between the form and characteristics of urban government and leadership, and its performance. While mayors are often visible on a national and global stage, a centralised, one-tier system of city government with a strong mayor in charge is not a silver bullet for creating effective city leadership. Democracy is an important factor but, again, city-wide elections are not a solution on their own. Overall there was a great deal of discontent with the performance of local government. In close to half of the cities we surveyed, experts said that the structure of urban governance is either partly or entirely ineffective in addressing local challenges. This dissatisfaction with the structural set-up of city leadership cut across cities with one-tiered, two-tiered and pluralised systems.

This, to us, hints at the need to tailor city governance to local needs and local dynamics, rather than simply searching for an ideal 'model' of leadership. The exact mix of actors, structures and tools that will create effective leadership in a city will vary. The key to success is not in a formula, or model, but a locally tailored combination that balances these three elements. The key to effective city leadership, then, is not about the right mayor, the perfect plan, the reformed city council, but about the way all the elements of city leadership come together, interact and create something that is greater than the sum of its parts.

City leadership is embedded in a globalised world

Traditional outlooks on urban leadership and governance tend to focus on the city, or the urban region, as the primary geographical unit of analysis. Challenges and solutions are taken as being largely local in nature. Yet as chapter 4 highlighted, the challenges facing cities, and the capacity of urban leadership and governance to address these, are shaped by more than local issues. Cities, even smaller ones, are often influenced by national, regional and trans-national drivers, from macroeconomic trends, to political conflicts and environmental change. Poverty and inequality, environmental sustainability and effective governance were all cited as key challenges for the cities we studied. While local factors certainly play an important role in creating these challenges, clearly these are not just local concerns. The 2008 global financial crisis, for example, has had a profound impact on city leadership and governance, in particular on the fiscal health of cities.

At the macro-level, the twin drivers of urbanisation and globalisation are reshaping the geography of world politics and global markets. Cities are increasingly embedded in regional and global flows of capital, people and ideas. This has been combined with a relative decline, in many locations, of the welfare state's control of many aspects of social life. At the same time, from a 'micro' level, civil society and individual non-governmental initiatives have progressively risen to the forefront as key drivers of everyday economics and politics. As Denters and Rose (2005: 2) put it in an early-2000s review of city politics in the twentieth century, cities have been faced with substantial shifts in both 'their external socio-economic and broader political environments' while also being 'confronted with changes in the nature of their local communities'. Local governments have to respond to the challenges that arise from growing interconnectedness.

This is not to say that cities are at the mercy of exogenous, external forces. The way challenges manifest in cities is the result of the complex interplay between localised dynamics and global pressures. Solutions, then, need to be both locally embedded but also informed by practices elsewhere. To this end, cities are increasingly seeking to capitalise on this growing international connectivity by advocating for themselves and developing solutions at an international level. The growing number of national and international city networks focusing on issues from climate change to health attests to this (Acuto, 2016). City networks enable city leaders to learn from one another and plan jointly through the institutionalisation of forums and the promotion of policy mobility (McCann, 2011) via events, campaigns and joint projects. As studies (e.g. Bulkeley et al., 2003) have shown, networks have an effective impact on policy formulation and implementation, and play an important role in connecting leaders and accelerating local (and increasingly international) change. Practitioners in international planning have already recognised, perhaps even more explicitly than scholars, how city-to-city cooperation is an extremely important tool for city leadership. This cooperation allows them to share technical know-how and develop tools and structures beyond those normally available to local government to implement their plans (Keiner and Kim, 2007).

Despite the growth in city-to-city networking and international trans-urban outreach, our research found that the tools that cities use are still very local in nature. Our review of strategic urban plans, which we demonstrated are one of the most common tools of city leadership, found that while links downward to more localised plans were common, links upward to national and international agendas were not. Similarly, our review of the actors taking part in SUPs found that this tended to be a very localised group of people. This approach needs to be updated to ensure that SUPs, as a tool of city leadership, account for the profound impact that national and transnational events, flows and actors have on cities.

The future of city leadership: a need for reflection

This book has argued for a multi-dimensional, global approach to studying the process of city leadership. It is natural for a broad, comparative study such as this to raise more questions than it answers and we recognise that there is much more work to be done. Our aim has been to encourage greater reflection on city leadership, in terms of what it is, how it operates and how it can respond to the diverse and complex challenges faced by cities around the world.

Going forward, both practitioners and scholars must work to reflect on and assess the experience of city leadership, and the lessons that can be learned, by drawing on a broad range of cities. City leaders and the other elements of city leadership often embrace ambitious visions and plans. Unfortunately, all too often these plans are not completed and become the victim of resource shortages, bureaucratic inefficiencies, corruption and the constraints that a short political cycle places on achieving long-term objectives. As with any level of government, a legacy of promises that are not delivered upon weakens city leadership. However, failures of leadership can be more immediately evident and catastrophic at the city level than at other levels because of the role of local government in delivering the services that people rely on in their everyday lives.

Despite the crucial role of city leadership in the well-being of the majority of the world's population, it is surprising that city leadership and how it can be improved are not 'hot topics' in scholarship on urban issues. Neither the New Urban Agenda, for instance, nor the Sustainable Development Goals, focus on the evaluation of old and new governance structures or tools. Since Habitat III, there has been a great deal of debate on the interface between science and policy, or academics and local governments. Evaluating current models of leadership and governance, and developing evidence-based suggestions for improving these, are one of the more significant contributions that academia and research institutions could make to support cities to achieve the SDGs.

Evidence-based assessments, both comparative as we have tried to do here and more localised studies, will be fundamental to understand the current state of city leadership around the world and how to improve it. From a methodological standpoint, one challenge will be to balance the need for comparative work while still providing localised and policy-relevant insights. A core component of future scholarship must be a recognition that ideas and solutions will come from many different places. Knowledge sharing follows many trajectories and scholars must take care not to make assumptions about where the ideas worth sharing come from. In our research, no clear distinctions emerged about the better 'performers', in terms of leadership, between the Global North and South. In fact, certain regions that might be traditionally thought of as 'developing' might have much to teach the Global North. For example, our research found that the Latin America and Caribbean region has a much higher proportion of women in leadership roles.

This leads us to advocate, even more firmly than at the outset of the project and the book, for greater global attention to the dynamics of urban governance. The role of leadership in creating urban policy, directing urban development and reconciling everyday urban needs with global aspirations must be better appreciated by scholars and practitioners alike.

Appendices
Appendix 1: List of cities that were included in the survey

City	Country
Aberdeen	UK
Abidjan	Ivory Coast
Abu Dhabi	UAE
Abuja	Nigeria
Accra	Ghana
Addis Ababa	Ethiopia
Adelaide	Australia
Alexandria	Egypt
Alice Springs	Australia
Algiers	Algeria
Amman	Jordan
Amsterdam	Netherlands
Ankara	Turkey
Antananarivo	Madagascar
Astana	Kazakhstan
Athens	Greece
Atlanta	USA
Auckland	New Zealand
Austin	USA
Baguio	Philippines
Baku	Azerbaijan
Bangalore	India
Bangkok	Thailand
Barcelona	Spain
Baton Rouge	USA

(Continued)

City	Country
Beijing	China
Beirut	Lebanon
Belfast	UK
Belgrade	Serbia
Berlin	Germany
Bilbao	Spain
Bogotá	Colombia
Bologna	Italy
Boston	USA
Brasilia	Brazil
Brighton	UK
Brisbane	Australia
Brussels	Belgium
Bucharest	Romania
Budapest	Hungary
Buenos Aires	Argentina
Bulawayo	Zimbabwe
Busan	South Korea
Cairo	Egypt
Calgary	Canada
Cali	Colombia
Canberra	Australia
Cape Coast	Ghana
Cape Town	South Africa
Caracas	Venezuela
Carmel-by-the-Sea	USA
Changwon	South Korea
Chennai	India
Chicago	USA
Christchurch	New Zealand
Copenhagen	Denmark
Cordoba	Spain
Curitiba	Brazil
Dakar	Senegal
Dar Es Salaam	Tanzania
Delhi	India

(Continued)

City	Country
Denver	USA
Detroit	USA
Dhaka	Bangladesh
Dili	Timor-Leste
Doha	Qatar
Dubai	UAE
Dublin	Ireland
Fatick	Senegal
Florence	Italy
Frankfurt	Germany
Freetown	Sierra Leone
Gaborone	Botswana
Gorakhpur	India
Guadalajara	Mexico
Guayaquil	Ecuador
Harare	Zimbabwe
Havana	Cuba
Ho Chi Minh City	Vietnam
Hong Kong	China
Houston	USA
Huancayo	Peru
Ibadan	Nigeria
Innsbruck	Austria
Islamabad	Pakistan
Istanbul	Turkey
Jakarta	Indonesia
Jeddah	Saudi Arabia
Jerusalem	Israel
Johannesburg	South Africa
Kansas City	USA
Karachi	Pakistan
Khartoum	Sudan
Kingston	Jamaica
Kinshasa	Democratic Republic of Congo
Kisumu	Kenya
Kolkata	India

(Continued)

City	Country
Kraków	Poland
Kuala Lumpur	Malaysia
Kumasi	Ghana
Kuwait City	Kuwait
La Paz	Bolivia
Lagos	Nigeria
Lahore	Pakistan
Leuven	Belgium
Lima	Peru
Liverpool	UK
Lomé	Togo
London	UK
Los Angeles	USA
Luxembourg	Luxembourg
Lyon	France
Macao	China
Madrid	Spain
Malé	Maldives
Managua	Nicaragua
Manaus	Brazil
Manchester	UK
Manila	Philippines
Maputo	Mozambique
Maringá	Brazil
Medellin	Colombia
Melbourne	Australia
Mexico City	Mexico
Miami	USA
Milan	Italy
Minsk	Belarus
Mogadishu	Somalia
Monrovia	Liberia
Montreal	Canada
Moscow	Russia
Mumbai	India

(Continued)

City	Country
Munich	Germany
Nairobi	Kenya
New Orleans	USA
New York	USA
Nicosia	Cyprus
Nuuk	Greenland
Osaka	Japan
Panama City	Panama
Paramaribo	Suriname
Paris	France
Perth	Australia
Philadelphia	USA
Phnom Penh	Cambodia
Port Moresby	Papua New Guinea
Port of Spain	Trinidad and Tobago
Port-au-Prince	Haiti
Portland	USA
Prague	Czech Republic
Punta Arenas	Chile
Putrajaya	Malaysia
Qingdao	China
Quito	Ecuador
Recife	Brazil
Reykjavik	Iceland
Rio de Janeiro	Brazil
Riyadh	Saudi Arabia
Rome	Italy
Saint Petersburg	Russia
San Francisco	USA
San Juan	Puerto Rico
San Salvador	El Salvador
Santiago de Chile	Chile
Santo Domingo	Dominican Republic
São Paulo	Brazil
Seattle	USA

(Continued)

City	Country
Seoul	South Korea
Shanghai	China
Singapore	Singapore
Skopje	Macedonia
Stockholm	Sweden
Strasbourg	France
Surat	India
Sydney	Australia
Taipei	Taiwan
Tehran	Iran
Tel Aviv	Israel
Tirana	Albania
Tokyo	Japan
Toronto	Canada
Tripoli	Lebanon
Tromsø	Norway
Turin	Italy
Ulaanbaatar	Mongolia
Urumqi	China
Valencia	Spain
Valparaiso	Chile
Vancouver	Canada
Vatican City	Vatican
Venice	Italy
Vienna	Austria
Villavicencio	Colombia
Warsaw	Poland
Washington DC	USA
Waterloo	Canada
Wellington	New Zealand
Wuhan	China
Xalapa	Mexico
Yellowknife	Canada
Zanzibar	Tanzania
Zurich	Switzerland

Appendix 2: List of Strategic Urban Plans reviewed in-depth

Plan	City/Region	Country	Region
City of Adelaide Strategic Plan 2012–2016	Adelaide	Australia	East Asia and Pacific
The 20-Year Plan for Greater Adelaide			
Hong Kong: 2030 Planning Vision and Strategy	Hong Kong	China	
Kuala Lumpur Structure Plan 2020	Kuala Lumpur	Malaysia	
Ulaanbaatar Master Plan 2020	Ulaanbaatar	Mongolia	
Urban Development Strategy	Christchurch	New Zealand	
Concept Plan 2011 and MND's Land Use Plan	Singapore	Singapore	
Greenest City 2020 Action Plan	Vancouver	Canada	Europe and North America
Metro Vancouver 2040			
Vision 2030: A Guide to the Future	Stockholm	Sweden	
Zurich Strategies 2025	Zurich	Switzerland	
Aberdeen City and Shire Strategic Development Plan	Aberdeen	UK	
Manchester's Local Development Framework	Manchester	UK	
Stronger Together: Greater Manchester Strategy 2013			
Detroit Future City	Detroit	USA	
Strategic Plan Rio de Janeiro Municipal Government 2013–2016	Rio de Janeiro	Brazil	Latin America and Caribbean

(Continued)

Plan	City/Region	Country	Region
Development Plan 2012–2016	Bogotá	Colombia	
City Hall Strategic Plan 2008–2015	Santo Domingo	Dominican Republic	
Sustainable Port of Spain Trinidad and Tobago Action Plan	Port of Spain	Trinidad and Tobago	
Metropolitan Caracas Strategic Plan 2020	Caracas	Venezuela	
Strategic Development Plan for Greater Cairo Region 2050	Cairo	Egypt	**Middle East and North Africa**
Strategic Plan for Tel Aviv Yafo	Tel Aviv	Israel	
Plan Abu Dhabi 2030	Abu Dhabi	UAE	
Karachi Strategic Development Plan 2020	Karachi	Pakistan	**South and Central Asia**
Strategy for Socio-Economic Development for St Petersburg until 2030	St Petersburg	Russia	
Lagos State Development Plan 2012–2025	Lagos	Nigeria	**Sub-Saharan Africa**
Kigali Master Plan Report	Kigali	Rwanda	
The Joburg 2040 Growth and Development Strategy	Johannesburg	South Africa	
City of Harare Strategic Plan 2012–2025	Harare	Zimbabwe	

References

Acuto M, 2016, 'Give cities a seat at the top table', *Nature* 537: 611–13
Acuto M, 2018, 'Engaging with global urban governance', in Harrison J and Hoyler M (Eds) *Doing Global Urban Research*. London: Sage, 96–109
Acuto M and Parnell S, 2016, 'Leave no city behind', *Science* 352(6288): 873
Acuto M, Parnell S and Seto K C, 2018, 'Building a global urban science', *Nature Sustainability* 1(1): 2–4
Acuto M and Rayner S, 2016, 'City networks: breaking gridlocks or forging (new) lock-ins?', *International Affairs* 92(5): 1147–66
Ahrend R, Gamper C and Schumann A, 2014, 'The OECD Metropolitan Governance Survey', Organisation for Economic Co-operation and Development, Paris, http://www.oecd-ilibrary.org/content/workingpaper/5jz43zldh08p-en
Albrechts L, 2004, 'Strategic (spatial) planning reexamined', *Environment and Planning B: Planning and Design* 31(5): 743–58
Albrechts L, 2006, 'Bridge the gap: From spatial planning to strategic projects', *European Planning Studies* 14(10): 1487–1500
Albrechts L, Healey P and Kunzmann K R, 2003, 'Strategic spatial planning and regional governance in Europe', *Journal of the American Planning Association* 69(2): 113–29
Amano T, González-Varo J P and Sutherland W J, 2016, 'Languages are still a major barrier to global science', *PLOS Biology* 14(12) e2000933
Angel S, Parent J, Civco D L, Blei A and Potere D, 2011, 'The dimensions of global urban expansion: Estimates and projections for all countries, 2000–2050', *Progress in Planning* 75(2): 53–107
Asian Development Bank, 1999, 'Asian cities in the 21st century: contemporary approaches to municipal management', Asian Development Bank, Manila, Philippines, http://www.adb.org/sites/default/files/publication/27897/vol1roman.pdf
Avolio B J, 2007, 'Promoting more integrative strategies for leadership theory-building', *American Psychologist* 62(1): 25–33
Avolio B J, Bass B M and Jung D I, 1999, 'Re-examining the components of transformational and transactional leadership using the Multifactor Leadership', *Journal of Occupational and Organizational Psychology* 72(4): 441–62
Avolio B J, Walumbwa F O and Weber T J, 2009, 'Leadership: Current theories, research, and future directions', *Annual Review of Psychology* 60(1): 421–49
Barnett C and Parnell S, 2016, 'Ideas, implementation and indicators: Epistemologies of the post-2015 urban agenda', *Environment and Urbanization*, 28(1): 87–98.
Bass B M, 1990a, *Bass & Stogdill's Handbook of Leadership: Theory, Research, and Managerial Applications*. London: Simon and Schuster
Bass B M, 1990b, 'From transactional to transformational leadership: Learning to share the vision', *Organizational Dynamics* 18(3): 19–31
Bass B M, 1995, 'Theory of transformational leadership redux', *The Leadership Quarterly* 6(4): 463–78
Bass B M, 1997, 'Does the transactional–transformational leadership paradigm transcend organizational and national boundaries?', *American Psychologist* 52(2): 130–39
Bassett K, 1996, 'Partnerships, business elites and urban politics: New forms of governance in an English city?', *Urban Studies* 33(3): 539–55
Baum-Snow N and Pavan R, 2012, 'Inequality and city size', *The Review of Economics and Statistics* 95(5): 1535–48

Beer A and Clower T, 2014, 'Mobilizing leadership in cities and regions', *Regional Studies, Regional Science* 1(1): 5–20

Bénit-Gbaffou C and Katsaura O, 2014, 'Community leadership and the construction of political legitimacy: Unpacking Bourdieu's "political capital" in post-apartheid Johannesburg', *International Journal of Urban and Regional Research* 38(5): 1807–32

Bennett N, Wise C, Woods P A and Harvey J A, 2003, *Distributed Leadership*. Nottingham: National College of School Leadership

Bennis W, 2007, 'The challenges of leadership in the modern world: Introduction to the special issue', *American Psychologist* 62(1): 2–5

Berg R and Rao N, 2005, 'Institutional reforms in local government: A comparative framework', in Berg R and Rao N (Eds) *Transforming Local Political Leadership*. Basingstoke: Palgrave Macmillan, 1–14

Billing Y D and Alvesson M, 1989, 'Four ways of looking at women and leadership', *Scandinavian Journal of Management* 5(1): 63–80

Bloomberg M, 2015, 'City Century: Why municipalities are the key to fighting climate change', *Foreign Affairs*, 94(2): 116

Bolden R, 2011, 'Distributed leadership in organizations: A review of theory and research', *International Journal of Management Reviews* 13(3): 251–69

Bolden R, Gosling J, Marturano A and Dennison P, 2003, 'A review of leadership theory and competency frameworks', Centre for Leadership Studies, University of Exeter, https://ore.exeter.ac.uk/repository/handle/10036/17494

Bolden R and Kirk P, 2006, 'From leaders to leadership', *Effective Executive* 8(10): 27–33

Borraz O and John P, 2004, 'The transformation of urban political leadership in Western Europe', *International Journal of Urban and Regional Research* 28(1): 107–20

Bremmer I, 2015, 'The absence of global leadership will shape a tumultuous 2016', *Time*, 21 December 2015, at: http://time.com/4154044/geopolitics-2016/

Bryson J M and Roering W D, 1987, 'Applying private-sector strategic planning in the public sector', *Journal of the American Planning Association* 53(1): 9–22

Bryson J M, 2001, 'Strategic planning', in Smelser N J and Baltes P B (Eds) *International Encyclopedia of the Social and Behavioral Sciences*. Oxford: Pergamon, 15, 145–151

Bryson J M, 2003, 'Strategic planning and management', in Peters G and Pierre J E (Eds) *Handbook of Public Administration*. Thousand Oaks, CA: Sage, 38–47

Bull H, 2012, *The Anarchical Society: A Study of Order in World Politics*. Basingstoke: Palgrave Macmillan

Bulkeley H and Betsill M, 2005, 'Rethinking sustainable cities: Multilevel governance and the "urban" politics of climate change', *Environmental Politics* 14(1): 42–63

Bulkeley H and Castán Broto V, 2013, 'Government by experiment? Global cities and the governing of climate change', *Transactions of the Institute of British Geographers* 38(3): 361–375.

Bulkeley H, Davies A, Evans B, Gibbs D, Kern K and Theobald K, 2003, 'Environmental governance and transnational municipal networks in Europe', *Journal of Environmental Policy & Planning* 5(3): 235–54

Bussu S and Bartels K P R, 2014, 'Facilitative leadership and the challenge of renewing local democracy in Italy', *International Journal of Urban and Regional Research* 38(6): 2256–73

C40 and Arup, 2015, *Potential for Climate Action*. London: C40 Cities Climate Leadership Group and ARUP

Caprotti F, Cowley R, Datta A, Broto V C, Gao E, Georgeson C, Herrick N, Odendaal D and Joss S, 2017, 'The New Urban Agenda: key opportunities and challenges for policy and practice', *Urban Research & Practice*, 10(3): 367–78

Carless S A, 1998, 'Gender differences in transformational leadership: An examination of superior, leader, and subordinate perspectives', *Sex Roles* 39(11–12): 887–902

Carmona M (Ed.), 2009, *Planning through Projects : Moving from Master Planning to Strategic Planning – 30 Cities*. Amsterdam: Techne Press

Cilliers P, 1998, *Complexity and Postmodernism: Understanding Complex Systems*. London: Routledge.

Cities Alliance, 2006, 'Guide to City Development Strategies: Improving Urban Performance', Cities Alliance, Washington, DC, http://www.citiesalliance.org/node/737

Clark G and Moir E, 2015, 'Density: drivers, dividends and debates', London: Urban Land Institute

Clark G, Moonen T, Moir E and Mountford D, 2015, 'Local Economic Leadership', Organisation for Economic Co-operation and Development, Paris, http://www.oecd.org/cfe/leed/OECD-LEED-Local-Economic-Leadership.pdf

Collinge C and Gibney J, 2010, 'Connecting place, policy and leadership', *Policy Studies* 31(4): 379–91

Collinge C, Gibney J and Mabey C, 2010, 'Leadership and place', *Policy Studies* 31(4): 367–78

Conley D T and Goldman P, 1994, 'Facilitative leadership: How principals lead without dominating', *OSSC Bulletin* 37(9), http://eric.ed.gov/?id=ED379728

Copus C, 2008, 'English councillors and mayoral governance: Developing a new dynamic for political accountability', *The Political Quarterly* 79(4): 590–604

Curtis S, 2016, 'Cities and global governance: State failure or a new global order?', *Millennium*, 44(3): 455–77

Curtis S, 2018, 'Global cities and the ends of globalism', *New Global Studies*, 12(1): 75–90

Dachler H and Hosking D M, 1995, 'The primacy of relations in socially constructing organizational realities', in Hosking D M, Dachler H and Gergen K J (Eds) *Management and Organization: Relational Alternatives to Individualism*. Aldershot: Avebury, 1–29, http://psycnet.apa.org/psycinfo/1996-97352-000

D'Alessandro C and Léautier F, 2016, *Cities and Spaces of Leadership: A Geographical Perspective*. London: Springer

Deas I, 2014, 'The search for territorial fixes in subnational governance: City-regions and the disputed emergence of post-political consensus in Manchester, England', *Urban Studies* 51(11): 2285–314

Deas I, Hincks S and Headlam N, 2013, 'Explicitly permissive? Understanding actor interrelationships in the governance of economic development: The experience of England's Local Enterprise Partnerships', *Local Economy* 28(7–8): 718–37

Denhardt R B and Denhardt J V, 2003, 'The new public service: an approach to reform', *International Review of Public Administration* 8(1): 3–10

Denis J-L, Lamothe L and Langley A, 2001, 'The dynamics of collective leadership and strategic change in pluralistic organizations', *Academy of Management Journal* 44(4): 809–37

Denters S A and Rose L E, 2005, *Comparing Local Governance. Trends and Developments*. Basingstoke: Palgrave Macmillan.

Dienesch R M and Liden R C, 1986, 'Leader-member exchange model of leadership: A critique and further development', *Academy of Management Review* 11(3): 618–34

Digaetano A and Klemanski J S, 1999, *Power and City Governance: Comparative Perspectives on Urban Development*. 1st ed. Minneapolis: University of Minnesota Press

Dinh J E, Lord R G, Gardner W L, Meuser J D, Liden R C and Hu J, 2014, 'Leadership theory and research in the new millennium: Current theoretical trends and changing perspectives'. *The Leadership Quarterly* 25 (1): 36–62

Dobbs R, Smit S, Remes J, Manyika J, Roxburgh C and Restrepo A, 2011, 'Urban world: Mapping the economic power of cities', McKinsey Global Institute, http://www.mckinsey.com/global-themes/urbanization/urban-world-mapping-the-economic-power-of-cities

Dodson J, 2017, 'The global infrastructure turn and urban practice', *Urban Policy and Research* 35(1): 87–92

Downs A, 2005, 'Smart growth: Why we discuss it more than we do it', *Journal of the American Planning Association* 71(4): 367–78

Easterly W, 2015, 'The trouble with the sustainable development goals', *Current History*, 114(775): 322

Economist, The 2015, 'The 169 commandments', *The Economist*, https://www.economist.com/news/leaders/21647286-proposed-sustainable-development-goals-would-be-worse-useless-169-commandments

Elcock H, 2008, 'Elected mayors: Lesson drawing from four countries', *Public Administration* 86(3): 795–811

Evans M, 2014, 'Democracy, legitimacy and local government electoral reform', *Local Government Studies* 40(1): 41–63

Fenwick J and Elcock H, 2005, 'The elected mayor and local leadership', *Public Money & Management* 25(1): 61–6

Fiedler F E, 1967, *Theory of Leadership Effectiveness*. New York: McGraw-Hill

Florida R, 2014, 'Cost of living is really all about housing', *CityLab*, http://www.citylab.com/housing/2014/07/cost-of-living-is-really-all-about-housing/373128/

Friedmann J, 2004, 'Strategic spatial planning and the longer range' *Planning Theory & Practice* 5(1): 49–67

Gains F, Greasley S, John P and Stoker G, 2007, 'Does leadership matter? A summary of evidence on the role and impact of political leadership in English local government', Department for Communities and Local Government, London, https://www.escholar.manchester.ac.uk/uk-ac-man-scw:68229

Gibney J, Copeland S and Murie A, 2009, 'Toward a "new" strategic leadership of place for the knowledge-based economy', *Leadership* 5(1): 23

Goldsmith M, 2001, 'Urban governance', in Paddison R (Ed.) *Handbook of Urban Studies*, London: Sage, 325–35

Gordon, D J and Johnson C A, 2017, 'The orchestration of global urban climate governance: Conducting power in the post-Paris climate regime', *Environmental Politics* 26(4): 694–714

Graen G B and Uhl-Bien M, 1995, 'Relationship-based approach to leadership: Development of leader-member exchange (LMX) theory of leadership over 25 years: Applying a multi-level multi-domain perspective', *The Leadership Quarterly* 6(2): 219–47

Greasley S and Stoker G, 2008, 'Mayors and urban governance: Developing a facilitative leadership style', *Public Administration Review* 68(4): 722–30

Greasley S and Stoker G, 2009, 'Urban political leadership', in Davies J S and Imbroscio D L (Eds) *Theories of Urban Politics*. 2nd ed. London and Los Angeles: Sage, 125–36

Grint K, 2012, 'Elected Mayors and City Leadership: Summary report of the third Warwick commission', Warwick: University of Warwick, https://www2.warwick.ac.uk/research/warwickcommission/electedmayors/summaryreport/the_warwick_commission_on_elected_mayors_and_city_leadership_summary_report.pdf

Gronn P, 2000, 'Distributed properties: A new architecture for leadership', *Educational Management Administration & Leadership* 28(3): 317–38

Guastello S J, 1995, 'Facilitative style, individual innovation, and emergent leadership in problem solving groups', *The Journal of Creative Behavior* 29(4): 225–39

Gurran N and Bramley G, 2017, *Urban Planning and the Housing Market: International Perspectives for Policy and Practice*. London: Springer

Hambleton R and Howard J, 2013, 'Place-based leadership and public service innovation', *Local Government Studies* 39(1): 47–70

Hambleton R and Sweeting D, 2004, 'U.S.-style leadership for English local government?', *Public Administration Review* 64(4): 474–88

Hardoy J E, Mitlin D and Satterthwaite D, 1992, *Environmental Problems in Third World Cities*. London: Earthscan

Haselmayer S, 2018, 'The de-globalized city', *New Global Studies*, 12(1): 65–73

Healey P, 1997, *Collaborative Planning: Shaping Places in Fragmented Societies*. Basingstoke: Macmillan

Healey P, 2002, 'On creating the "city" as a collective resource', *Urban Studies*, 39(10): 1777–92

Healey P, 2007, *Urban Complexity and Spatial Strategies: Towards a Relational Planning for Our Times*. London: Routledge

Heifetz R A, 1994, *Leadership Without Easy Answers*. Cambridge, MA: Harvard University Press

Heifetz R, Grashow A and Linsky M, 2009, 'Leadership in a (permanent) crisis', *Harvard Business Review* 87(7/8): 62–9

Hemphill L, McGreal S, Berry J and Watson S, 2006, 'Leadership, power and multisector urban regeneration partnerships', *Urban Studies* 43(1): 59–80

Henshilwood E and Cullinan M, 2012, *Leveraging Density: Urban Patterns for a Green Economy*. Nairobi, Kenya: UN-Habitat

Hersey P, Blanchard K H and Johnson D E, 2007, *Management of Organizational Behavior*. 9th ed. Upper Saddle River, NJ: Prentice Hall

Hord S M, 1992, 'Facilitative Leadership: The Imperative for Change', Washington, DC: United States Department of Education, http://eric.ed.gov/?id=ED370217

Horner M, 1997, 'Leadership theory: past, present and future', *Team Performance Management: An International Journal* 3(4): 270–87

Hosking D M, 1988, 'Organizing, leadership and skilful process[1]', *Journal of Management Studies* 25(2): 147–66

Hosking D M, 2007, 'Not leaders, not followers: A post-modern discourse of leadership processes', in Shamir B, Pillai M, Bligh M and Uhl-Bien M (Eds) *Follower-centered Perspectives on Leadership: A Tribute to the Memory of James R. Meindl*. Greenwich, CT: Information Age Publishing, 243–63

Howard J and Sweeting D, 2007, 'Addressing the legitimacy of the council-manager executive in local government', *Local Government Studies* 33(5): 633–56

Iles P and Preece D, 2006, 'Developing leaders or developing leadership? The Academy of Chief Executives' programmes in the North East of England', *Leadership* 2(3): 317–40

Jago A G, 1982, 'Leadership: Perspectives in theory and research', *Management Science* 28(3): 315–36

Jogulu U and Ferkins L, 2012, 'Leadership and culture in Asia: the case of Malaysia', *Asia Pacific Business Review* 18(4): 531–49

Johnson C A, 2017, *The Power of Cities in Global Climate Politics: Saviours, Supplicants or Agents of Change?* London: Palgrave Macmillan.

Jonas A E G and Ward K, 2007, 'Introduction to a debate on city-regions: new geographies of governance, democracy and social reproduction', *International Journal of Urban and Regional Research* 31(1): 169–78

Kearns A and Paddison R, 2000, 'New challenges for urban governance', *Urban Studies* 37(5–6): 845–50

Keiner M and Kim A, 2007, 'Transnational city networks for sustainability', *European Planning Studies* 15(10): 1369–95

Kemeny T, 2013, 'Immigrant diversity and economic development in cities: a critical review', Spatial Economics Research Centre (SERC), London: London School of Economics and Political Science, http://www.spatialeconomics.ac.uk/SERC/publications/default.asp

Kennedy J C, 2002, 'Leadership in Malaysia: Traditional values, international outlook', *The Academy of Management Executive (1993-2005)* 16(3): 15–26

Khanna P, 2016, *Connectography: Mapping the Future of Global Civilization*. New York: Random House.

Kickert W J M and Klijn E-H, 1997, 'A management perspective on policy networks', in Kickert M, Klijn E-H and Koppenjan J F M (Eds) *Managing Complex Networks: Strategies for the Public Sector*. London and Thousand Oaks, CA: Sage, 1–13

Kjær A M, 2004, *Governance*. Malden, MA: Polity/Blackwell

Kooiman J, 2003, *Governing as Governance*. London: Sage

KPMG, 2016, 'Future State 2030' *KPMG*, https://home.kpmg.com/xx/en/home/insights/2015/03/future-state-2030.html

Liden R C, Sparrowe R T and Wayne S J, 1997, 'Leader-member exchange theory: The past and potential for the future', *Research in Personnel and Human Resources Management* 15: 47–120

López Moreno E, Orvañanos Murguía R and Lavagna G, 2015, 'City Prosperity Index: 2015 Global City Report', Nairobi, Kenya: UN-Habitat, https://unhabitat.org/wp-content/uploads/2016/02-old/CPI_2015%20Global%20City%20Report.compressed.pdf

Lowndes V and Skelcher C, 1998, 'The dynamics of multi-organizational partnerships: an analysis of changing modes of governance', *Public Administration* 76(2): 313–33

LSE Cities, 2014, 'Governing Urban Futures: Data' London: LSE Cities, https://lsecities.net/publications/conference-newspapers/governing-urban-futures-data/

Marshall A, 2004, 'Europeanization at the urban level: Local actors, institutions and the dynamics of multi-level interaction', *Journal of European Public Policy* 12(4): 668–86

Mastop H and Faludi A, 1997, 'Evaluation of strategic plans: the performance principle', *Environment and Planning B: Planning and Design* 24(6): 815–32

McCann E, 2011, 'Urban policy mobilities and global circuits of knowledge: Toward a research agenda', *Annals of the Association of American Geographers* 101(1): 107–30

McKinsey & Company, 2013, 'How to make a city great', http://www.mckinsey.com/insights/urbanization/how_to_make_a_city_great

McPhearson T, Parnell S, Simon D, Gaffney O, Elmqvist T, Bai X, Roberts D and Revi A, 2016, 'Scientists must have a say in the future of cities', *Nature*, 538(7624): 165

Mines M and Gourishankar V, 1990, 'Leadership and individuality in South Asia: The case of the South Indian Big-man', *The Journal of Asian Studies* 49(04): 761–86

Montero A P and Samuels D, 2004, 'The political determinants of decentralization in Latin America: Causes and consequences', in Montero A P and Samuels D (Eds) *Decentralization and Democracy in Latin America*. Notre Dame, IIN: University of Notre Dame Press, 3–34

Mossberger K and Stoker G, 2001, 'The evolution of urban regime theory: The challenge of conceptualization', *Urban Affairs Review* 36(6): 810–35

Mouritzen P E and Svara J H, 2002, *Leadership at the Apex: Politicians and Administrators in Western Local Governments*. Pittsburgh: University of Pittsburgh Press

Naidu J and Van der Walt M S, 2005, 'An exploration of the relationship between leadership styles and the implementation of transformation interventions', *SA Journal of Human Resource Management* 3(2): 1

Newman P, 2008, 'Strategic spatial planning: Collective action and moments of opportunity', *European Planning Studies* 16(10): 1371–83

Newman P and Thornley A, 2011, *Planning World Cities: Globalization and Urban Politics*. 2nd ed. Basingstoke and New York: Palgrave Macmillan

Northouse P G, 2012, *Leadership: Theory and Practice*. 6th ed. Thousand Oaks, CA: Sage

OECD, 2015, *Governing the City* (Organisation for Economic Co-operation and Development, Paris), http://www.oecd-ilibrary.org/content/book/9789264226500-en

OECD, 2014, OECD Regional Outlook 2014. Regions and Cities: Where Policies and People Meet, Paris: Organisation for Economic Co-operation and Development, http://www.oecd-ilibrary.org/urban-rural-and-regional-development/oecd-regional-outlook-2014_9789264201415-en

Ogilvie F and Goodman A, 2012, 'Inequalities in usage of a public bicycle sharing scheme: Socio-demographic predictors of uptake and usage of the London (UK) cycle hire scheme', *Preventive Medicine* 55(1): 40–5

Oosterlynck S, Beeckmans L, Bassens D, Derudder B, Segaert B and Braeckmans L (Eds), 2018, *The City as a Global Political Actor*. London: Routledge

Palley M L, 2001, 'Women's policy leadership in the United States', *PS: Political Science and Politics* 34(2): 247–50

Palmer B, Walls M, Burgess Z and Stough C, 2001, 'Emotional intelligence and effective leadership', *Leadership & Organization Development Journal* 22(1): 5–10

Palumbo A, 2010, 'Governance: meanings, themes, narratives and questions', in Bellamy R and Palumbo A (Eds) *From Government to Governance*. Farnham: Ashgate, xi–xxx

Papa M J, Daniels T D and Spiker B K, 2007, *Organizational Communication: Perspectives and Trends*. Revised edition. Los Angeles: Sage

Papageorgiou C, 2009, 'Does trade and financial globalization cause income inequality?', *IMF Research Bulletin* 10(3)

Parnell S, 2016, 'Defining a global urban development agenda', *World Development*, 78: 529–40

Parnell S, 2018, 'Globalization and sustainable development: At the urban crossroad', *The European Journal of Development Research*, 30(2): 169–71

Parnreiter C, 2011, 'Commentary toward the making of a transnational urban policy?', *Journal of Planning Education and Research* 31(4): 416–22

Pierre J and Peters B G, 2000, *Governance, Politics and the State*. New York: Palgrave Macmillan, http://www.palgrave.com%2Fpage%2Fdetail%2Fgovernance-politics-and-the-state-jon-pierre%2F%3FK%3D9780333718483

Prentice W C H, 1961, 'Understanding leadership', *Harvard Business Review* 39(5): 143–51

Price M and Benton-Short L, 2007, 'Counting immigrants in cities across the globe', *migrationpolicy.org*, http://www.migrationpolicy.org/article/counting-immigrants-cities-across-globe

PricewaterhouseCoopers LLP, 2005, 'Cities of the future: global competition, local leadership', PricewaterhouseCoopers, https://www.pwc.com/gx/en/government-public-sector-research/pdf/cities-final.pdf

Purdue D, 2001, 'Neighbourhood governance: Leadership, trust and social capital', *Urban Studies* 38(12): 2211–24

Rada D R, 1999, 'Transformational leadership and urban renewal', *Journal of Leadership & Organizational Studies* 6(3–4): 18–33

Rapoport E, 2015, 'Globalising sustainable urbanism: the role of international masterplanners', *Area* 47 (2): 110–15

Rapoport E and Hult A, 2017, 'The travelling business of sustainable urbanism: International consultants as norm-setters', *Environment and Planning A: Economy and Space* 49(8): 1779–96

Revi A, 2016, 'Afterwards: Habitat III and the Sustainable Development Goals', *Urbanisation* 1(2): x–xiv

Rhodes R A W, 1996, 'The new governance: governing without government', *Political Studies* 44(4): 652–67

Rhodes R A W, 1997, *Understanding Governance: Policy Networks, Governance, Reflexivity, and Accountability*. Maidenhead: Open University Press

Ricci M, 2015, 'Bike sharing: A review of evidence on impacts and processes of implementation and operation', *Research in Transportation Business & Management* 15: 28–38

Robinson J, 2002, 'Global and world cities: a view from off the map', *International Journal of Urban and Regional Research* 26(3): 531–54

Savitch H and Vogel R K, 2009, 'Regionalism and urban politics', in Davies J S and Imbroscio D L (Eds) *Theories of Urban Politics.* 2nd ed. Los Angeles and London: Sage, 106–24

Schrank D, Lomax T and Eisele B, 2011, 'TTI's 2011 Urban Mobility Report', Texas A&M Transportation Institute, The Texas A&M University System, https://trid.trb.org/view.aspx?id=1122263

Scott A J (Ed.), 2001a, *Global City-Regions: Trends, Theory, Policy.* Oxford: Oxford University Press

Scott A J, 2001b, 'Globalization and the rise of city-regions', *European Planning Studies* 9(7): 813–26

Shatkin G, 2004, 'Globalization and local leadership: Growth, power and politics in Thailand's eastern seaboard', *International Journal of Urban and Regional Research* 28(1): 11–26

Simon, D, Arfvidsson H, Anand G, Bazaz A, Fenna G, Foster K, Jain G, Hansson S, Evans L M, Moodley N and Nyambuga C, 2016, 'Developing and testing the Urban Sustainable Development Goal's targets and indicators – a five-city study', *Environment and Urbanization* 28(1): 49–63

Slack E and Côté A, 2014, 'Comparative urban governance', United Kingdom Government Office for Science, London

Sotarauta M, 2016, *Leadership and the City: Power, strategy and networks in the making of knowledge cities.* Abingdon and New York: Routledge

Spillane J P, 2006, *Distributed Leadership.* Chichester: Wiley

Steinberg F, 2005, 'Strategic urban planning in Latin America: experiences of building and managing the future', *Habitat International* 29(1): 69–93

Stogdill R M, 1950, 'Leadership, membership and organization', *Psychological Bulletin* 47(1): 1–14

Stoker G, 1998, 'Governance as theory: five propositions', *International Social Science Journal* 50(155): 17–28

Stone C N, 1989, *Regime Politics: Governing Atlanta, 1946–1988.* Lawrence, KS: University Press of Kansas

Stone C N, 1995, 'Political leadership in urban politics', in Judge D, Stoker G and Wolman H (Eds) *Theories of Urban Politics.* London: Sage, 96–116

Suchman M C, 1995, 'Managing legitimacy: Strategic and institutional approaches', *The Academy of Management Review* 20(3): 571–610

Svara J H, 2003, 'Effective mayoral leadership in council-manager cities: Reassessing the facilitative model', *National Civic Review* 92(2): 157–72

Swyngedouw E, 2004, 'Globalisation or 'glocalisation'? Networks, territories and rescaling', *Cambridge Review of International Affairs* 17(1): 25–48

Tannenbaum R, Weschler I and Massarik F, 1961, *Leadership and Organization.* New York: McGraw-Hill

Tavares R, 2016, *Paradiplomacy: cities and states as global players.* Oxford: Oxford University Press

Transparency International, 2016, 'Corruption Perceptions Index 2015' *www.transparency.org*, https://www.transparency.org/news/pressrelease/corruption_perceptions_index_2015_corruption_still_rife_but_2015_saw_pocket

Uhl-Bien M, 2006, 'Relational Leadership Theory: Exploring the social processes of leadership and organizing', *The Leadership Quarterly* 17(6): 654–76

Uhl-Bien M, Marion R and McKelvey B, 2007, 'Complexity Leadership Theory: Shifting leadership from the industrial age to the knowledge era', *The Leadership Quarterly* 18(4): 298–318

UN-Habitat, 2009, 'Planning Sustainable Cities: Global Report on Human Settlements 2009', Nairobi, Kenya: UN-Habitat, http://unhabitat.org/books/global-report-on-human-settlements-2009-planning-sustainable-cities/

UN-Habitat, 2011, 'State of the World's Cities 2010-2011: Bridging the urban divide', London and Washington, DC: Earthscan

UN-Habitat, 2014, 'A new strategy for sustainable neighbourhood planning: five principles. Urban Planning Discussion Note.' Nairobi, Kenya: UN-Habitat, https://unhabitat.org/a-new-strategy-of-sustainable-neighbourhood-planning-five-principles/

UN-Habitat, 2015, 'Housing and slum upgrading'. Nairobi, Kenya: UN-Habitat, http://unhabitat.org/urban-themes/housing-slum-upgrading/ (last accessed 7 December 2018)

UN-Habitat, 2016a, 'Housing for all', Nairobi, Kenya: UN-Habitat, https://unhabitat.org/books/housing-for-all-the-challenges-of-affordabilityaccessibility-and-sustainability/

UN-Habitat, 2016b, 'World Cities Report 2016', Nairobi, Kenya: UN-Habitat, https://unhabitat.org/books/world-cities-report/

UNHCR, 2016, 'Global Trends. Forced Displacement in 2016', UNHCR. Available at http://www.unhcr.org/globaltrends2016/

United Cities and Local Governments; World Bank, 2009, *Decentralization and Local Democracy in the World: First Global Report by United Cities and Local Governments 2008*. Washington, DC: United Cities and Local Government and the World Bank, https://openknowledge.worldbank.org/handle/10986/2609 License: CC BY 3.0 IGO

United Nations, 2015, 'The Millennium Development Goals Report 2015'. New York: United Nations

United Nations Conference on Trade and Development, 2016, 'Trade and Development Report, 2016', New York and Geneva: United Nations, http://unctad.org/en/pages/PublicationWebflyer.aspx?publicationid=1610

Vanderleeuw J, Jarmon C, Pennington M, Sowers T and Davis T, 2011, 'Economic development perspective and city leadership', *Urban Studies Research* 2011 e436290

Van Wart M, 2013, 'Administrative leadership theory: a reassessment after 10 years', *Public Administration* 91(3): 521–43

Verheul W J and Schaap L, 2010, 'Strong leaders? The challenges and pitfalls in mayoral leadership', *Public Administration* 88(2): 439–54

Verrest H, Moorcroft S and Mohammed A, 2013, 'Global urban development programmes and local realities in the Caricom-Caribbean: mismatches in needs and approach', *Habitat International*, 40: 258–67

Vishwanath A, Gan H S, Kalyanaraman S, Winter S and Mareels I, 2014, 'Personalised public transportation: A new mobility model for urban and suburban transportation', in *17th International IEEE Conference on Intelligent Transportation Systems (ITSC)*: 1831–36

Weiss, T G and Wilkinson R, 2014, 'Global governance to the rescue: Saving international relations?', *Global Governance* 20(1): 19–36

World Health Organization, 'WHO Global Age-Friendly Cities Project', http://www.who.int/ageing/projects/age_friendly_cities/en/

World Bank, 2017, 'Dominican Republic Overview', *The World Bank in Dominican Republic*, http://www.worldbank.org/en/country/dominicanrepublic/overview

Wright B E and Pandey S K, 2010, 'Transformational leadership in the public sector: Does structure matter?', *Journal of Public Administration Research and Theory* 20(1): 75–89.

Wu F and Zhang J, 2007, 'Planning the competitive city-region: The emergence of strategic development plan in China', *Urban Affairs Review* 42(5): 714–40

Yukl G, 1989, 'Managerial leadership: A review of theory and research', *Journal of Management* 15(2): 251–89

Zaleznik A, 1977, 'Managers and leaders: Are they different?', *Harvard Business Review* May-June: 67–8

Zhang Y and Feiock R C, 2010, 'City managers' policy leadership in council-manager cities', *Journal of Public Administration Research and Theory* 20(2): 461–476

Zinnbauer D, 2016, 'Corruption: Habitat III's Elephant in the Room', http://citiscope.org/habitatII/commentary/2016/02/corruption-new-urban-agendas-elephant-room

Index

Bold page numbers indicate figures, *italic* numbers indicate tables.

100 Resilient Cities project 31

Aberdeen 70
Abu Dhabi 45, 68
academic study of city leadership, challenges of 4
   see also research project
accountability to constituencies 35
   see also public accountability and participation
actors in city leadership 29, 30–1, 44–7, **46, 47, 48**
   challenges re. structures 48–55
   coordination with institutions 79–80, 88–91, **90, 91**
   strategic urban plans (SUPs) 79–80
Addis Ababa 72
Addis Ababa Action Agenda 2, 24
Adelaide 68, 74, 93
affordable housing 67–9
age-friendly cities 49, 66–7
agencies/tiers, coordination between 48–51
Algiers 69
Amman 68, 74
Amsterdam 49, 67
Antananarivo 66
appointment of leaders 45, 47
Astana 66
Atlanta 72

Baguio 68
Baku 69
Bangalore 69
Bangkok 66
Barcelona 70
Bass, B.M. 14
Beirut 52, 66
Belfast 45, 47
Berlin 40, 70
bicycle-sharing schemes 64
Bloomberg, Michael 2, 32, 51
Bogota 93
Bologna 70
Brasília 45
Bremmer, Ian 3
bribery in city leadership 52–4
Brisbane 69, 74
Brussels 66, 69

Bucharest 50, 52, 72
Budapest 54
Bulawayo 49, 66, 72
Busan 70, 71

Cairo 40
Calgary 67, 69
Cape Town 74
car-sharing schemes 64
Caracas 68
catalyst, leadership as 29, 57
challenges for city leadership
   connectivity 62–4
   consistency in 74
   diversity of city populations 64–7
   durability of governance priorities 80, 87
   economic vitality 70–2
   effective governance as unifying theme 62
   environmental sustainability 72–4
   housing 67–9
   inequality 65–6
   as local and global 62
   mobility 62–4
   research aims 59
   spatial planning 67–70
   survey most frequent mentions **60**
   sustainability 72–4
   top categories 61, *61*
   transport infrastructure 63–4
   unemployment 72
Changwon 67
Chicago 52
Christchurch 70
cities
   age-friendly 49, 66–7
   diversity of ix
   future, leadership of x
   as global force x–xi
   increased visibility of 1
   shapes and sizes of x
   strategic planning for x
Cities Alliance 79
citizen inclusion 43, 54–5
   strategic urban plans (SUPs) 80, 91–4, **92, 93, 94**
city leadership
   actors in 29, 44–7, **46, 47, 48**
   challenges between actors and structures 48–55
   complexity of, increase in 17
   consistencies across cities 55
   context of, importance of 35

effectiveness of structures in 42–4, **43,** 55–6, 56–7
evolution of, need for 21
facilitative leadership 27–8
financial constraints 51–2
future cities x
future for 100–2
gender of city leaders 45, **46,** 58
global agendas of 1–3
global urban governance and 22–5, **23,** 99–100
governance, importance to 48
governance models and ixv
from government to governance 17–19
increased visibility of 1
individuals as leaders 44, 97–8
institutions in 31–2
interactions of ix–x
international importance of 3
lack of definition and knowledge about 3
leadership not leaders 97–8
length of term served 47
local links 3
mandate of leaders 45, 47, **47**
multi-disciplinary perspectives 25
partnerships in 18
place, focus on 25–7
research into 27
structures and institutions of 29, 31–2, 36–42, **37, 40, 41**
studying, challenges of 4
tailored to local needs 98–9
theories of 27–9, 27–34, **29**
theories of leadership and 25–6
three elements of **29,** 29–33
titles of city leaders 45
tools of 30, 32–3
typology of city government structures 38
variety of roles in 59
see also challenges for city leadership; theories of leadership
city-regions 20
city-states 36–7
civic engagement 43, 54–5
civil society movements 23
climate change 1, 2, 3, 9, 24, 33, 44, 56, 59, 61, 65, 73, 74, 100
Climate Leadership Group (C40) 23, 36, 42, 51, 59, 72
community-based organisations 31
complexity
  leadership 29
  structures in city leadership 42–3
Complexity Leadership Theory (CLT) 16–17
congestion 62–3
connectivity as challenge for city leadership 62–4
consultation, public 54–5
context of city leadership, importance of 35
contingency model 14
cooperative arrangements 39
coordination
  actors and institutions 79–80, 88–91, **90, 91**
  between tiers/agencies 48–51
corruption 52–4, 58
crowdsourcing web platforms 33

D'Alessandro, C. 26
data gathering for research project 6–8
debt, international 71
decentralisation of governance 21, 35, 44, 49, 52–3
Delhi 69
demographic changes 66–7
Detroit 71
Dinh, J.E. 12, 14
disasters 1, 2, 24, 44, 70, 74
distributed leadership 16, 21, 28
diversity ix
  city populations 64–7
  government structures 39–40
Dubai 43, 63, 66
durability
  governance priorities 80, 87
  leadership structures and institutions 32

economic vitality of cities 70–2
elderly, needs of 49, 66–7
election of leaders 45
entity perspectives 15
environmental sustainability as challenge for city leadership 72–4
ethnic diversity in cities 66

facilitative leadership 27–8
federal countries 36–7
federal districts 37
Fiedler, F.E. 14
finance in SDGs 58
financial constraints in city leadership 51–2
fiscal autonomy 37
FixMyStreet 33
Florence 70, 71
food inequality 66
foreign investment 52
formality of leadership structures and institutions 32, 38–9
fraud in city leadership 52–4
future cities, leadership of x

Gaborone 54, 70
gender of city leaders 45, **46,** 58
geographies of governance 19–20
Germany 36–7
global cities 6, 9, 66
global urban governance
  agendas of city leaders 1–3, 56
  city leadership and 22–5, **23,** 35, 99–100
  coordination between city tiers/agencies 51
  economics, city 71
  global force, cities as x–xi
  international dimension of city leadership 22–5
  'scale jumping' 51
  strategic urban plans (SUPs) 96
global urbanisation, promise of ix
governance
  as challenge 36, **37**
  challenges effecting city leadership 48–55
  consistencies across citiies 55
  coordination between tiers/agencies 48–51
  corruption 52–4
  decentralisation 48

durability of priorities 80
effective as challenge for city leadership 62
financial constraints 51–2
geographies of 19–20
global urban, city leadership and 22–5, **23**
importance to city leadership 48
inclusiveness 43, 54–5
jurisdiction, institutional 50
leadership in context of 21–2
metropolitan tiers of government 50–1
mobility and 63–4
models, leadership and ix
moves towards in city leadership 17–19
national/local complexities 49
tailored to local needs 98–9
typology of city government structures 38
governor as title of city leaders 45
Graen, G.B. 13
Greasley, S. 28

Habitat III 2, 3
Hambleton, R. 21, 25-7, 28-9, 80
Havana 53
Hidalgo, Anne 1–2
Hong Kong 63, 66, 89
housing 67–9
Huancayo 68, 74

Ibadan 69
ICLEI Local Governments for Sustainability 59, 72
image of the city 70
immigrants 66
inclusiveness of governance systems 43, 54–5
  strategic urban plans (SUPs) 80, 91–4, **92, 93, 94**
individuals 44
  length of term 47
  mandate of leaders 45, 47, **47**
  as not leaders 97–8
  titles of city leaders 45
inequality
  access to transport 63
  in cities 65–6
  environmental issues and 73–4
informal settlements 69
information technology as tool for city leadership 33
institutional reforms 21–2
institutions in city leadership 29, 31–2, 36–42, **37, 40, 41**
  coordination with actors 79–80, 88–91, **90**
  jurisdiction 50
  strategic urban plans (SUPs) 79–80
instruments of city leadership *see* strategic urban plans (SUPs); tools of city leadership
integration in cities 66
interactions between leaders and others 13
international dimension of city leadership 22–5
  see also global urban governance
Islamabad 74
issues for city leadership *see* challenges for city leadership
Istanbul 70

Jeddah 69
Jerusalem 70
jurisdiction, institutional 50

Kansas City 52
Karachi 54
Kearns, A. 56
Kigali Master Plan Report 89
Kingston 71
Kisumu 69
Kuala Lumpur 63
Kumasi 53, 62, 66, 68, 69

Lagos 40
land distribution and management 68
language as issue in research project 9–10
leader-based approaches to leadership 14–15
Leader-Member Exchange (LMX) theory 15
leadership
  in context of governance 21–2
  leader-based approaches 14–15
  not leaders 97–8
  scholarly approaches to 11
  transactional/transformational 14
  see also city leadership; theories of leadership
Léautier, F. 26
legitimacy
  in local government 21–2, 31–2
  strategic urban plans (SUPs) 81–2
Leuven 74
Lima 52
local authorities as international partners 24
local leadership, focus on 21
London 39, 66, 98
Los Angeles 66
Luxembourg 52, 71
Lyon 66

Macau 71
Male 66
mandate of leaders 45, 47, **47**
Manila 39–40
Maputo 73
Maringá 62, 69
mayors 44
  as international actors 3
  as title of city leaders 45
mechanisms of city leadership *see* tools of city leadership
Melbourne 69
methodological challenges of research project 9–10
metropolitan government approach 20
metropolitan regions 19
metropolitan tiers of government 50–1, 52
Milan 69
military conflicts 66
Medellín 33
Minsk 52, 53, 70
mobility as challenge for city leadership 62–4
Monrovia 63
Munich 62

Nairobi 53, 68
nation states as urban actors 24–5
national context, city status in 40

national economy, cities and 71
national/local complexities 49
networks
  city **23**, 24, 36, 40, **41, 42**, 100
  environmental sustainability 72–3
  regional/international 22–5
  role of 18–19
New Orleans 72
New Urban Agenda 57, 96
New York 52, 54, 66, 74
Nicosia 63, 68
non-linearity of leadership 29

older people, needs of 49, 66–7
100 Resilient Cities project 31
one-tier systems 38, 39
Organisation for Economic Cooperation and Development (OECD) reports 20
Osaka 50, 52

Paddison, R. 56
Panama City 43
Paramaribo 63
Paris 50
Paris Conference on Climate Change 3, 24
Parnell, S. 2, 23, 53
participation in city leadership *see* public accountability and participation
partnerships in city leadership 18
Perth 71
philanthropy, growth of globally 24
physical planning, lack of 63
place-based leadership 25–7
  research into 27
  see also city leadership
planning
  physical, lack of 63
  spatial, as challenge for city leadership 67–70
  urban growth 68
pluralised systems 38, 39
polycentric perspective 20
population changes 66–7
Port-au-Prince 72
Port of Spain 62, 63
Portland 68, 70
private investment, growth of globally 24
process, leadership as a 13, 15–17, 28, 30
property, leadership as a 12–13, 14–15
public accountability and participation 43, 54–5
  strategic urban plans (SUPs) 80, 91–4, **92, 93, 94**
public transport 63–4
Purdue, D. 27

Quito Implementation Plan of the New Urban Agenda 57, 96

reforms, institutional 21–2
regeneration of city centres 70
regime theory 21
regional military conflicts 66
regional scale 19–20
  government structure 39, **40**
relationship-based approaches to leadership 15–17
research project
  aims 5–6
  breadth of 6, 10
  cities included **7**, 103–8
  collaborative links 5
  data analysis 8–9
  data gathering 6–8
  desk research 9
  experts, survey of 6–8, 10
  grouping of cities 6
  identification of experts 10
  international dimension of city leadership 9
  language as issue 9–10
  methodological challenges 9–10
  parallel study 9
  primary research 7–8
  secondary research 8
  selection of cities 6
  snowball sampling 8
  strategic plans reviewed 109–10
  see also challenges for city leadership
resilience-building 31
Rio de Janeiro 53, 54
Riyadh 54

San Francisco 54
Santo Domingo 71
'scale jumping' 51
Seattle 49
selection of leaders 45, 47
Sendai Framework 2, 24, 44
Slum Dwellers International 31
social inequality
  in cities 65–6
  environmental issues and 73–4
society, focus on 18, 19
spatial planning
  as challenge for city leadership 67–70
  in strategic urban planning 78
spatial segregation 65
State of World Cities 2016 report 49
Stockholm 54, 68, 73
Stoker, G. 28
strategic urban plans (SUPs) x, 32–3
  alignment with challenges 84–95, **88, 90, 91, 92, 93, 94**
  as commonly used tool 77
  coordination of actors and institutions 79–80, 88–91, **90, 91**
  defined 78–9
  durability of governance priorities 80, 87
  effectiveness of 83–4, **84**
  embeddedness 90–1
  global links, lack of 100
  impact, measurement of 96
  implementation as focus 81–2, 94–5
  international influences 79
  international landscape of 82–4, **83, 84**
  international scale 96
  legitimacy of 81–2
  limited set of issues 81
  links to other plans 89–90, **91**
  links with other levels of government 89
  monitoring and evaluation (M&E) 95
  non-governmental influences 79
  objectives in 87, **88**
  organisations leading **92**, 92–3

origin and development of approach 77–8
outputs from 78
participation in city leadership 80, 91–4, **92, 93, 94**
partners in process of **93**, 93–4, **94**
political change and 87
by region **83**
research focus on 76–7
research methodology 77
review of documents 85–6, *85–6*
revisions 81
spatial focus 78
timeframes 83
variety in style, focus and depth 82–3
structures in city leadership 29, 31–2, 36–42, **37, 40, 41**
challenges re. actors 48–55
complexity of 42–3
consistencies across citiies 55
effectiveness of 42–4, **43**, 55–6, 56–7
metropolitan tiers of government 50–1
new, working with other elements 56
study of city leadership, challenges of 4
see also research project
survey of cities
extent of xi
see also research project
sustainability as challenge for city leadership 72–4
Sustainable Development Goals (SDGs) 24, 57–8
Svara, J.H. 28
Sydney 62, 63

Taipei 71
theories of leadership
actors in city leadership 29, 30–1
catalyst, leadership as 29, 57
city leadership 27–9
and city leadership 25–6
complex and non-linear, leadership as 29
Complexity Leadership Theory (CLT) 16–17
defining leadership 12–13, 13
distributed leadership 16, 28
dominance of North America and Europe 12
facilitative leadership 27–8
as individuals, structures and institutions 28–9
institutions in city leadership 29, 31–2
interactions between leaders and others 13
Leader-Member Exchange (LMX) theory 15
process, leadership as a 13, 15–17, 28, 30
property, leadership as a 12–13, 14–15
relationship-based approaches 15–17
structures in city leadership 29, 31–2
three elements of city leadership **29**, 29–33
tools of city leadership 29, 30, 32–3
three elements of city leadership **29**, 29–33
tiers/agencies, coordination between 48–51
Tirana 64
titles of city leaders 45
tools of city leadership 29, 30, 32–3, 89
see also strategic urban plans (SUPs)
Toronto 63, 66
traffic congestion 62–3
transactional/transformational leadership 14

transnational initiatives 23
see also global urban governance
transparency, lack of 53
transport infrastructure 63–4
Tripoli 66, 68
Turin 72
two-tier systems 38, 39
typology of city government structures 38

Uhl-Bien, M. 13, 15, 16–17
United Cities and Local Governments (UCLG) 23, 42, 44, 53
unemployment 72
United Nations Framework on Disaster Risk Reduction 2, 24, 44
unemployment 72
United Nations Conference on Trade and Development (UNCTAD) 52
UN-Habitat 5, 49, 53, 54, 55, 65-6, 68-9, 78-80, 92
United States
federal districts 37
government structure 36
urban growth, planning for 68, 74
urban regime theory 21
urban renewal 70
urban sprawl 69, 74

Valencia 71
Valparaiso 53
Vancouver 50–1, 63, 73, 74

Warsaw 69
Washington DC 66, 74
water, drinking, shortage of 73
Wellington 63

Xalapa 63

Yellowknife 71
youth population of cities 66

Zanzibar City 68, 73
Zurich 53

www.ingramcontent.com/pod-product-compliance
Lightning Source LLC
LaVergne TN
LVHW050008140426
836100LV00010B/64